Musings

Sonal Thakur

authorHOUSE®

AuthorHouse™ UK Ltd.
500 Avebury Boulevard
Central Milton Keynes, MK9 2BE
www.authorhouse.co.uk
Phone: 08001974150

First published by AuthorHouse 12/27/2010.

ISBN: 978-1-4520-6453-6 (sc)

This book is printed on acid-free paper.

PREM KAHANI

On the perils of heartbreak and more!

Every woman who has suffered the loss of love or known heartbreak will know what I mean by the term 'temporary insanity'. I think we all do at some time go through it when we face the loss of a loved one, may be a spouse or a lover. Loss is faced with feelings of bereavement, grief, emptiness, and insecurity and life is never the same again.

This takes me back to a few remarkable scenes in the movie' Benares' where Urmila dresses up as a bride after she learns of the tragic death of her lover on the eve of her marriage. Another moving scene is the one where the disillusioned psychiatrist played by Akaash Khurana tries to tell her to move on with life as her lover is now dead and gone. And Urmila bangs away on the keys of her piano in anguish and claims that her lover is not dead and he will live in her heart forever.

A lot of women walked out of the theatre not having understood the film at all. Perhaps they had not been fortunate enough to experience that kind of love, which is earth shattering.

The diva Rekha always talks of her mystery lover who changed her life. True, we all know who that 'mystery lover' is but we will let Rekhaji maintain her mystery & enigma. We women since the time we are young girls are influenced by the men in our lives. Women also play a role but our femininity and our concept of who we are and how we relate to our world is defined by our fathers and later the other men in our lives. According to Freud, the father of psychoanalysis, boys suffer from what is known as Oedipus complex where they believe themselves to be in love with their mothers and see their fathers as competition. I don't think girls suffer from any such complexes and the father figure is always the provider and the protector. A girl's teenage years and her relationship with her father are critical to her self esteem and confidence.

Men and women have different roles to play, and it's true that society is changing with more women stepping out and earning the bread and butter. But I think, given a choice, a woman would be happy playing house if she has a satisfying and secure married life. Our traditional society does seem to be under threat with the very institution of marriage being questioned. In such a scenario, the prolific writer and media personality Ms Shobhaa De came out with her book 'Spouses' which is a must read for all people either married or considering marriage. It explores the good and the bad of married life, talking about several situations that one deals with in marriage. My personal favourites would have to be the chapter titled 'Dumbing Down' where an intelligent woman plays dumb so that she does not appear smarter than her husband!

An article in the Sunday TOI recently talked about alpha women—the new powerful woman who is a super achiever. These words were quoted by Shahrukh Khan—'Alpha or beta women are still women and we should love them'. I say, we need more men like Shahrukh Khan!

I had an arranged marriage, and my husband from Bihar who is an MBA from the US treated me like a second class citizen. It was an eye-opener to me that while women have moved way ahead in their thinking, some men still live in the dark ages. They simply do not understand the concept of equality of the sexes. Some men I know are so threatened by their wives' sexuality that if they find her too responsive in bed they label her a slut. Other men are so inspired by what they see on the pornographic sites, and whose experience of women is limited to what they see on these sites, behave quite crazily in bed. Some of them are inspired by group sex and threesomes and foursomes, some by the same sex, and some others get a kick out of lesbian sex. We have movies today on wife swapping and some others on lesbian relationships etc. I think people look for such diversions because they are frankly incapable of the emotion of love and do not have any satisfying relationships in their lives. According to me, sex is best when it is between man and woman, one on one, and it is within a safe committed relationship. Live in relationships are also being tried out, but I think in most cases they are due to economic and practical considerations, and if for some reason it doesn't work out, then, as always, the woman is the loser.

I believe that to some extent the use of pornography and erotica to spice up one's love life is not bad as it helps to keep the excitement alive. Some people believe that sex gets boring in a relationship after some time. I think that's ridiculous. There was a film in which the lead actress lost her husband of twenty years. And when her friend asks her what she missed the most she says that it was the routine of their lives and their sex life together that she missed the most. She said that everything worked like clockwork and one knew exactly what would happen after what and that was a great source of comfort and security—the routine of their sex lives.

A lot of people still think of sex as taboo. Frankly, sex is natural and fun. It improves your immunity, releases happiness hormones, and gives you an overall sense of well being. Not to mention the calories you lose after a good workout!

When Ms Shobhaa De came out with her novels, people found them to be too racy and sexually explicit. I think she was very bold to write about sex as it is part and parcel of our lives. Khushwant Singh also writes racy novels about sex. There is something called creative license. Just because these people write about sex, it does not mean they are lecherous sleaze balls in their personal lives. People need to lose their fear of sex.

Actresses of today, especially the bold and brash Mallika Sherawat and Bipasha Basu, have literally ignited the imagination of millions of movies goers with their sexy, steamy scenes on the big screen. They are both women with beautiful bodies and they are not afraid to flaunt them. They are women comfortable with their sexuality and it shows on the screen. Bipasha has a remarkable face and Mallika a remarkable body. In fact, in the movie 'Shaadi Se Pehle' she is a show stealer and sizzler. Mallika's lines in her first movie 'Khwaaish' were indeed a little shocking, but quite teasing when she declares to her lover, 'I want your naked body next to mine'.

The much awaited sequel of Basic Instinct hit the screen this year. It's a once in a lifetime role for Sharon Stone and the woman is really amazing. You can actually hear everybody suck in their breath in the movie theatre when she appears on the screen. Unfortunately the censor board has cut all the juicy scenes for the Indian audiences and you don't get to see much skin on display.

I think if a woman looks after herself, she can continue to look beautiful and desirable long after her prime. If Sharon Stone can look hot at fifty, so can Rekha or Hema Malini. In fact, Rekha would be my choice to play Sharon Stone in the desi version of Basic Instinct as I feel she is the ultimate seductress. Who can forget her in Silsila and Umrao Jaan. Hema Malini had all the younger heroines running for cover in Baghban.

Aishwarya Rai is another indisputable beauty, and the highlights of her career would be 'Shaabd' and 'Kajra Re'. She looks gorgeous and one cannot take one's eyes away from her. British critics have panned her film 'Mistress of Spices' saying that she is a beauty without sensuality. How further from the truth could they be!

The latest blockbusters 'Dhoom II' and 'Umrao Jaan' should silence her critics once and for all as she is indeed a luminous beauty.

Sex in the 21st Century

Talking about erotic literature and pornography, the capital, Delhi, has a lot to offer in such terms. There are tiny bookshops at PVR Saket and Priya that sell the most interesting and varied collection of books. There are romance novels the all time favourite star comics and old issues of the Cosmopolitan and Vogue offering valuable tips on how to improve your sex life. There is erotica titled,' The Happy Hooker' by an anonymous author and other such tales of adult love and passion. As a child one sometimes came across erotic literature lying around the house and it was inconceivable to us that our normal, boring parents could indulge in such stuff. A prying, nosy, curious child that I was I would find some stuff hidden in the corner of my parents cupboard, and as a teenager I would satisfy my curiosity when nobody was around. I once came across some small stone figurines depicting the poses at the Khajuraho Temple. May be my parents had picked them up on a trip to Khajuraho. Anyway, that my parents were passionate and madly in love with each other was no secret. As my father often said, 'Love is hot like the summer' (When asked to define love].

Delhi also boasts of cyber cafes that have the latest clips from the cyber world on display. One would find a new picture on the desktop everyday and one would know what the flavour of the day was, be it Sania Mirza or Jessica Alba or the then JLo.

There would be interesting clips doing the rounds such as one on a lookalike of Sania Mirza in Cincinnati making out with a young stud.

There was another one of a scene on a metro rail in Japan where

5

two commuters start feeling each other up in a crowded train quite oblivious to the rest of the world. There was another one of a rape scene of Monica Belluci, which was quite graphic and revolting. The world of the web can expose you to things that you would not see in your normal life. Women as a rule I don't think enjoy pornographic stuff. It is more a male indulgence. But, yes, once you are married, you do get exposed to it as your husband may keep copies of the Playboy magazine or may indulge in watching pornography. It comes as a shock initially, but one gradually gets accustomed to it.

A strange phenomenon has now taken over with SMS and Internet chat. Sex is available at a message and people make friends on the Internet and let all inhibitions down under the guise of anonymity. Somehow, I think it is a good thing to a certain extent with a lot of lonely, old, divorced, and frustrated people finding love and romance on the Net and finding an outlet for their fantasies which could otherwise face social censorship.

Speed dating is another New Age concept, but give me good old-fashioned romance anytime!

Inhibitions in society have certainly come down with young women experimenting with sex and indulging in casual sex, occasionally. Virginity somehow doesn't seem to be such a valued commodity. But, I think, given a choice, a man would prefer that his wife was chaste and pure. A real man will always cringe at the thought of his wife having been with someone else. Similarly, for a woman to know that her partner is clean makes a big difference to a relationship. Somehow in the U.S.A. where teenagers earlier had sex at the age of twelve and fourteen, young school girls are now taking the vows of virginity and trying to save their love for the right man.

Disillusioned with love I had come to believe that Mr Right doesn't exist, and we just have to make do with what we have. But I think if we believe in dreams, we can make them come true.

THE BIRDS AND THE BEES

An essay on the perils of being an independent woman in today's world!

Another issue that needs to be seriously addressed is that of rape. Now that women are stepping out of their homes more and are more sexually expressive, they should be careful about how they are in the presence of men and what kind of attention they attract. When I was in college, awareness regarding sex was very limited. I think it would be a fact to say that I had absolutely no knowledge of the birds and the bees and our mothers were too tight lipped about these things. Whatever we learnt was mainly misinformation from friends and books. Nor were the T.V. channels as explicit about sexual matters as they are in today's time and age. When I joined Sophia, Mumbai for my graduation, I was quite confused and lost about these matters. There were a lot of young women on campus and in the hostel who were in relationships and would tell us about their experiences. There was immense conflict within the soul as to what was right and what was wrong.

People ask me if I remember my first kiss. I certainly do. It was a pretty yucky affair. Often, our first sexual encounter can leave us with feelings of guilt and can give you a feeling of being dirty and unclean. Young women are often quite ignorant about sexual matters and get lured into relationships by young, over sexed men. For a woman sex most often has to do with love, whereas for a man sex is just that—sex!

We have often heard of the term date rape. Rape is often perpetrated by people we know—acquaintances, boyfriends, neighbours, relatives, etc. Even in a relationship, if a man crosses his limits or forces the woman into doing something she is unwilling to do, it should be considered as rape. Women should be careful not give mixed signals. Marital rape is when a husband forces himself onto a wife who is unwilling.

Sexual attraction is very crucial to the working of a relationship. It bonds two people as man and woman is a strange unexplainable thing. It is nothing short of magic.

People often say that they do not believe in love at first sight. It think it can happen in the first glance only. You see a person and you know that you were meant to be. There is that instant attraction, the spurt of recognition. If you have to click with someone, it could happen in an instant and if it doesn't have to work you can wait a lifetime and it will never work. The say we all have a love map within us that guides us to the person of our dreams. We all have an image in our minds as to what Mr Right or Ms Right should be like. It is based on our experiences as children and also on the memory of the people we meet in our life that may have influenced us while we were growing up, such as fathers, mothers, uncles, aunts, cousins, friends, etc. When we find a person who fits our love map, viola! That magical thing called love happens!

Sati, dowry deaths, rape, and other atrocities against women have not ceased. But I do feel they have abated. In today's day and age, women should be financially independent as it empowers a woman. Men will not stop abusing women. It is the women who have to put their foot down against the abuse. They have to say no and have the courage to walk out of bad marriages, relationships, and other exploitative situations. Society can often be unkind to single women, but women should reach out to each other and form a support system and find a voice and identity for themselves.

After separating from my husband, all my credit cards and other documents required a change of name. Most of the men I encountered seemed very uncomfortable doing it and they asked me all kinds of prying and probing questions. I flatly told them if I wanted to use my maiden name was that a problem? The idea that a woman could discard her husband's name and seek an identity for herself seemed inconceivable to them. It seemed very threatening and unnatural to them.

I honestly believe women should retain their maiden names even after marriage. I mean it's the identity you have grown up with and it is who you are. To expect a woman to submerge her identity into her man after marriage is difficult. A lot of women I know experience a total loss of identity after marriage. They give up their careers, their lives, their names, and their individualities for the sake of marriage and for the social and economic security. All I can say is that it's not an easy transition to make, and I have come across many women on the verge of a breakdown as a result of all the compromises and adjustments they have had to make.

Destination New Delhi

Delhi's transition from walled city to world city!

As one lands in the capital, New Delhi, one is confronted by the new slogan coined by TOI, which says 'from walled city to world city'. Delhi as a city has truly arrived on the global scene. It has highways, satellite towns, monuments, history, art and culture, fashion, food, beautiful people, and of course the politicians!

As a city, it is completely alive with events and happenings galore. While I was there in February 2006, Delhi was celebrating. It's 'Chalo Delhi' festival. There were hot balloon races, fairs, and fetes galore. The 5th of March, International Women's Day, saw an event at India Gate where Mrs Sheila Dixit and Renuka Chowdhary inaugurated a movement to save the girl child. Shibani Kashyap and Usha Uthup regaled the audiences with their melodious and powerful voices and songs. And then there was the Indian Fashion Week with all the Hoopla and the Hype.

Multiplexes in Delhi screen the latest Hollywood movies; Munich, Da Vinci Code, Basic Instinct II, Memories of a Geisha are just a few noteworthy ones I had the opportunity to watch. Fashion in Delhi is amazing, with Janpath, G.K. Market, Karol Bagh, and Lajpath Nagar being some of my favourites. One can find a wide range of the most mind boggling stuff ranging from clothes, shoes, bags, belts, purses, and you name it at affordable prices. Again, food is available in plenty. The Qutub Institutional Area where I lived had vendors selling mouth-watering *aloo-parathas* and *chola* for just Rupees seven. It was simply unthinkable! It is a student area and *thalis* are available for just Rupees fifteen and non-vegetarian food for a mere twenty Rupees.-. Even at the height of the chicken-flu panic, people on the roadside were devouring chicken and eggs like it was nobody's business!

One does see a lot of disparity in wealth in Delhi as well. On the one hand you have service apartments in the exclusive Qutub Hotel going for Rupees two lakhs per month. On the other, hand you have a man selling drinking water for 50 paisa per glass just outside the hotel, and nobody seems to find this strange. You have young street kids selling newspapers and flowers on the streets of Delhi. I happened to be returning home one evening and a man was selling books at a traffic signal. It was almost 9 in the night and I had my last hundred Rupee note in my pocket. Something made me give this man the money. He broke into a relieved smile and said, 'I have been on the street since eight in the morning and this is my first sale for the day. Thank you!' I was moved. I would often go to PVR Priya and Saket to catch a movie and there would be beggars and rag pickers. I would ask them how much they made in a day and they would say about Rupees twenty. I asked them what they did with the money. They said they gave it to their parents. Something to think about!

A meal at a good hotel in Delhi costs about Rupees eight hundred. In the meanwhile, the rickshaw pullers on the road still chargeRupees fifteen- and Rupees twenty for a short ride. It is becoming increasingly difficult for me to understand this disparity. On the one hand there is an immense upward mobility among the people. You often encounter people on the road talking of deals of not less than hundred crores. And you stop and think! And, then, you see these fancy restaurants with bright lights and well dressed people talking and laughing, and just outside the restaurant you see a homeless family huddling together in the cold and the dark.

I am no Mother Teresa, but if I declared at a beauty contest that I would like to help the poor, I would really mean it. In our country, people seem to be desensitized towards poverty. They believe that they have a right to be rich, whereas the poor deserve to be poor.

Everyone has the right to happiness and the basics of existence such as food, shelter, and drinking water. It's time we did something about the poor of our country and only then would we be entitled to be called a progressive nation.

I was working briefly at the Indian Institute of Planning and Management in Delhi. They claim to be the largest B-School in India, currently challenging the position of the IIM's. They have international faculty of repute teaching at the institute. They give free laptops to students and also an educational trip to Europe. One of the first things I did on joining was to read Arindam Chaudhuri the founder's, book 'The Great Indian Dream'. He sounds very idealistic in his book, but frankly, I think the poor are a mere statistic in his book. He talks about India having an India centric economic policy but I don't see that happening. Sewagram at Wardha, a medical college, encourages its students to do a one year internship in the rural area. Why can't these management schools do the same? Do the students in Delhi and other cities really know what the real India is all about? The maverick guru, as he is called, also highly praises Gandhianism but one sees a stark materialistic attitude in their own personal and professional lifestyles. It's time they did some rethinking. What say?

The Metrosexual Man

An essay on the man of today and a brief mention of some of them who make it all happen!

Has the new age Indian man arrived? Well I think he is getting there, he is waking up to the new age women around him and making the necessary adjustments and changes. They are now watching women gyrating on the television sets in skimpy clothing. They probably have girlfriends who wear those kinds of clothes. There was a time when if a woman's bra peeked from under her clothes it was the greatest sin possible. But, now–a-days, you have fancy bra straps available in the market that you are proudly meant to display on your shoulders. Quite a change, really! How does the new age man adjust to these changes, Frankly, he doesn't have a choice, as the women are going to have their way, anyway.

The metrosexual man is conscious about his appearance, well dressed, and not afraid to show his feminine side. Saif Ali Khan would be a true example of a metrosexual man. A lot of men shy away from marriage and feel it robs them of their masculinity. Frankly, there is nothing more appealing than a married man—ask the ladies! And they say the most masculine thing a man can do is to become a father.

Indian men are, however, too tied to their mother's apron strings. And Indian women tend to spoil their sons silly. When a man gets married, he expects the same kind of pampering from his wife. Sorry to let you down guys, but it just doesn't work that way! You get as much as you give. And another piece of advice for men: keep a healthy distance from your moms once you get married and have a wife. There is nothing more putting off for a woman than to see a grown man cuddle up to his mother! Sorry mothers, but wives should come first!

Jemina Khan made a statement after her divorce to Imran Khan. She said, 'I was married for ten years and now I am having some fun. I think married couples should really take time away from responsibilities to have some fun. All work and no play can make a marriage boring and dull. Demands of the modern life are such that a lot of couples today have working relationships where the husband is in another place and the wife manages things in another. The pressures of a career keeps them apart. They share a long distance relationship, meeting occasionally to spend some time together. Metrosexual men have learnt to adjust and make compromises with marriage.

I have compiled a list of the few sexiest men we have in the country today. They would be in no particular order.

1.   **Karan Johar:** Young and successful film director with some mega hits to his credit. His chat show 'Coffee with Karan' was brilliant with him extracting some true confessions from his star guests. His witty and perceptive statements really had us laughing. A man really in touch with his feminine side and it shows in his tear-jerking films. His movie 'KANK' was real masterpiece.

2.   **Bikram Saluja:** An actor of exceptional good looks who has done cameo roles in films. His role as Karishma's boyfriend in Fiza was quite memorable. He played a bad guy in Page 3. We would certainly like to see him in some good meaty roles.

3.   **Shiamak Davar:** A hugely talented dancer who runs a very popular dance academy. He choreographs dances for major

movies And has an electric stage presence himself, not to mention a very elastic body. A star in his own right!

4.   **Dhoni:** The boy from Ranchi who made it big overnight on the international cricketing scene. His wild locks and savage looks have the women screaming for more. His statement that he drinks milk before matches only adds to his legendary status.

5.   **Hritik Roshan:** A rubber body, great moves, amazing biceps, and a remarkable good looker. This man is perfection personified. You just cannot get bigger than this. This guy is huge.[No pun intended!]

6.   **Abhishek Bachchan:** After having made a shaky start and gradually emerging from his father's shadow this young man was certainly the most sought after bachelor in the country till he decided to tie the knot with his lady love Aishwarya, in what was touted as the most watched event in the country.. Despite his sexy image, he has also established himself as an actor with stellar performances in Yuva, Bunty and Babli, Sarkar, Bluff Master, Dostana to name a few of his recent successes.

7.   **John Abraham:** Simple, yet tough, he is the guy next door. He also, has an amazing physique. His performance in 'Taxi no. 9211' was good. He is quite lucky to have gorgeous Bipasha as his girlfriend. A hot couple.His beach body and his' butt' show in Dostana had the nation panting!

8.   **Milind Soman:** A total sex-symbol who can forget the controversial Tuff shoes ad with Madhu Sapre—both in the buff with only a python wrapped around them! Has been the complete bachelor, not showing signs of slowing down. However, if rumours are to be believed he is marrying a French actress.

9. **Zulfi Syed:** A model known for his underwear ads, yet cute and eye candy. A guy you could take home to mamma minus the underwear. He looked nice in the movie Taj Mahal. Worth a dekko.

10. **Praful Patel:** A very savvy and debonair politician. Has single-handedly turned the aviation industry around. He is one of the coolest politicians we have around. A total page three regular.

11. **Rahul Gandhi:** With genes and a lineage like that anyone would be hot. A prospective prime minister in the making. But he still has a long way to go.

12. **Amitabh Bachchan:** Some men are hot all their lives. This man has shown no signs of aging or slowing down. The superstar of the millennium who has a wax statue at Madame Taussauds dedicated to him wins all the popularity votes hands down. A humble, simple man, yet flashy and funny, he has wooed audiences over the years. The man is an icon and is irreplaceable. No list would be complete without him.

13. **Gulzar:** Humble, simple in his *payjama-kurta,* yet a gifted poet of deep sensibilities. Men like him are rare.

14. **Mohinder Amarnath:** A soft-spoken gentleman, sober and good looking, who applied the same principles in the game of cricket. Low-key and therein lies his appeal.

15. **Prahalad Kakkar:** Ad guru, witty, humorous, tongue in cheek. Seen hanging out with young, hot babes in parties. Yet, he comes across as a family man and is quite harmless and likeable, really.

16. **Anil Ambani:** India's most successful businessman. Shrewd, sharp and quite good looking, too. Has good business instincts and that works for us ladies.

17. **Nana Patekar:** They say there is method in madness. Mad, schizophrenic, and hyper is how I would describe him. The masses love him and can identify with his angst.

The last three slots are left for the three Khans, Amir, Shahrukh and Salman. But a lot has already been said and spoken about them, so I am not going to say anymore.

Relevance of Mahatma Gandhi

Questioning the relevance of the Mahatma and his resurrection post Munnabhai!

It is quite ironical that some of the best Indian things came to us from the west and are probably more popular in the western world than they are in our own country. It took a Sir Richard Attenborough to capture the essence and greatness of this frail Mahatma. It is quite sad how he is a much neglected and condoned figure in our society. That the preaching of the Mahatma is relevant for all times is beyond a doubt. His theory of non-violence and *satyagraha* could not have been conceived by anyone else. Who else would have the courage to turn the other cheek when slapped on one? His struggle for the immigrant population in South Africa, his eventual return to India to merge himself into the turbulent politics of that time, and his struggle for social justice and equality have greatly placed him on a pedestal

He challenged the British government and had the empire quaking in fear of the Indian movement for independence, single-handed.

In today's time and age it is important that we recall the great sacrifices and heroic deeds of this great man. Gandhiji will always stand for truth, and truth is an eternal value. It can never lose its relevance or significance.

Those who think of Gandhiji's teachings as outdated and irrelevant to our times need to seriously rethink some issues. He is very much a part of the Hindu values of tolerance, forgiveness, sacrifice, and love for our neighbours. These values are part and parcel of the

Hindu psyche and character. They can and should not go out of fashion.

The box office hit film 'Munnabhai MBBS' brought a forgotten icon out of the closet and made the public rethink his beliefs and ideologies. It gave way to some introspection and some soul searching among some of his hardest critics who live in times of materialism and naked consumerism and globalization. These tough times only stressed the need for some balance and sanity, which are the essence of some of the values the Mahatma stood for.

It took the cheeky ignorance of a lovable thug to bring Gandhiji back to life in the film. The thug was an everyday character film audiences could identify with and the sublime message of the Mahatma came through in a simplified manner. Hence, it can be safetly said that every icon needs to be repackaged and reintroduced to every new generation.

There is a furore in India every time we see an international brand using the Mahatma to market its goods, be it a famous pen brand or a footwear company or then a misplaced meat brand. We make a noise and a ruckus trying to defend our icon, but exactly how respected and sanctified is he in our own backyard.

Recently, when his belongings came up for auctioning in the US, Indians made a hysterical claim to establish ownership of those items. That Vijay Mallya, the business tycoon, finally bid for them and bought them to the homeland is another matter. He has a private ownership of these collectibles, but the fact that they are in the custody of an Indian national gives much succour to a lot of ruffled hearts.

The Joy of Reading Newspapers

Can books survive the Internet onslaught?

The morning newspaper is like an addiction. Like the early morning cup of *chai*, one cannot do without the newspaper. It instantly connects you to the rest of the world. Reading it is a slow leisurely activity that has an art of its own. People fight over the newspaper, they loathe sharing it, and some even take it to the loo where they can spend hours just chewing over as a cow chews its cud. A newspaper gives you food for thought. It's our daily dose of news, views, and happenings. Newspaper reading is a hard habit to break, with people swearing by the same brand for years. Brand loyalty is very strong in the newspaper business. There is a fixed place for every item—the editorial, news, stock market, film reviews, matrimonial, to-lets, situations, vacant, etc., etc.

A lot of people made a fuss saying that television and Internet would kill the newspaper. It has become the age of instant gratification and people no longer have the time to read through the physical copy.

But the newspaper is one habit that is hard to break and will certainly not be replaced, come what may. The fine print scores over loud T.V. announcements and Internet clicking. The fine print has a lure of its own and will keep seasoned journalists hard at work and the reader hooked for life.

Freedom

On the importance of being free!

I think what a person needs above all else is freedom in their lives. Freedom to make the choices they do, freedom to love whom they choose to love, and freedom to be who they want to be. There is an old destitute woman in my colony who has been living on the street for many years now. One day, I approached her and told her to come with me and that I would take her to the old age home... 'There, they will clothe you and feed you and you will have a roof over your head', I told her. The old woman took one look at me and ran for her life. I still see her on the street, rummaging for food in garbage cans, wild unkempt hair and tattered clothes and all that. One finds her roaming the marketplaces begging the vendors for fruits etc. But I realise that she doesn't beg-she literally demands. She has a strange crazed look on her face but she looks happy and she looks free.

Sometimes, I observe poor people and beggars on the streets and I wonder if they are very sad or unhappy. Strangely, they are neither. They have their spirits about them and they go through the rigour of life with cheerfulness and laughter. I bought some kids ice creams at PVR Saket in Delhi and the little brats just snatched the cones from my hand and ran away. Here I was left standing like a fool, feeling very happy with myself and expecting words of thank you. That day, I realized that happiness is a right that everyone has privy to. Some rich people think they have the right to be rich and the poor deserve to be poor. They say the poor are lazy and do not work and hence they are on the streets. But, I also do not see some very rich working. Poverty is a vicious cycle and as the rich child is

21

born with the proverbial silver spoon in their mouth, the poor are also born with their disadvantages.

I think Ms Shobhaa De' is a very smart lady and often sympathetically comments on the poor of the society—the maid working for her, the *diya* seller during Diwali, etc. She, however, flaunts a real designer lifestyle in the most expensive clothes and jewellery. I would only like to ask her, 'Do you think that in a country where there is so much poverty, people should be flaunting such excess in their lifestyles?' We all like designer homes and designer lifestyles, but should we go overboard. Do we really need ten cars lined up in our driveway when we can make do with may be two? I have never been able to understand the naked pursuit of material things. Can money really buy happiness?

I feel sorry especially for the dispossessed during festivals, especially Diwali. In this time and age the festival of Diwali has become such a vulgar display of wealth. It is a festival for the rich when Goddess Lakshmi the goddess of wealth is worshipped. I really wonder how the poor must feel when they don't even have the money to buy oil to light lamps outside their homes.

Talking about freedom, another issue that appals me is that of killing in the name of love. When one reads of stories in the media about young people being done to death because they committed the crime of falling in love, I am shocked. These cases happen mostly in the states of U.P., Bihar, and Haryana. Every human being has the right to choose who they want to love and spend their lives with. It is a basic human right. And no one can take that away from you.

Faces and the stories they tell.

On reading people and interpreting their lives.

People gracefully develop, very interesting faces and personalities as they grow older. The lines, wrinkles, and their weathered skin tell a story. I often watch people and I find that their faces have a story to tell. Some women in particular look very graceful and beautiful as they grow older.

Women are, however, paranoid about growing older. But I believe that if they look after themselves and lead a healthy stress free life, they will only look more beautiful as they grow older. Experience teaches us a lot in life and the experiences we have lived make and shape our personalities.

A spiritual guru once said, 'aim for the wholeness of the soul and not for the soleness of the whole'. We should always aim for higher perfection and this perfection comes from knowledge and insights into life, which one develops through life's experiences.

A lot of women when asked what they do for a living say with quite an embarrassed air that they are just housewives. Women should stop being embarrassed about being housewives. The work they do at home is equally important and critical to the well being of the people who inhabit the house. The emotional and physical well being of the family is in their hands and they execute their task to full credit.

Never as good as the first time

Films, actresses, and goddesses, a businessman of steel and then some farmers, that make a complete world!

I recently watched a movie titled 'In Good Company', which deals with the issue of older employees being displaced by younger ones. It is a recent phenomenon where we see men in their twenties and early thirties taking over as CEOs of companies and, often, older men find themselves dealing with a younger boss–a situation they find rather difficult to deal with.

When the younger man in the movie asks his older colleague the secret of his successful family life, the older man played by Dennis Quaid says, 'You find the best person to share your fox hole with and when out of your fox hole, just keep your dick safely inside your trousers.' Ha! Ha! How well put !

I am quite a movie buff and I try to catch up on whichever good film that may be running in town. Lately, I found myself in a real catch 22 situation when I was faced with the dilemma of choosing between a Pierce Brosnan action thriller and a Rowan Atkinson British howler. May one never be faced with such a dilemma.

I think what really works for a film is a great script. All credit must go the script writer if the film works. Intelligent, perceptive dialogue really makes a good film. Page 3, the much acclaimed film by Madhur Bhandarkar, had some real hard hitting dialogues that left you impressed. I would rate Madhur Bhandarkar as one of the finest directors among the youth brigade, one who makes very realistic and hard hitting films. Taxi No. 9211 was again one of the better films of 2006. The angst of the failed taxi driver and the frustration of the young heir played by John Abraham and the chemistry between the two takes one back to some of the finest portrayals in Hollywood where the protagonist cracks up after years of battling the system.

A lot of films on serial killers and psychopaths show them to be extremely intelligent and gifted people who have either had an abusive childhood or are the victims of a corrupt system and society.

Nicole Kidman, Charlize Thereon, and Angelina Jolie are some of the incomparable beauties of Hollywood. Nicole Kidman is certainly a very fine and versatile actress who can play a wide variety of roles ranging from the dumb blonde of Bewitched to the seductress of Moulin Rouge.

Padma Lakshmi, the sexy wife of Salman Rushdie, who is a model actress, cook book writer, television presenter, and U.N. ambassador, was recently chosen by Newsweek Magazine for their cover, on a story about the new emerging India. They believed that she represented the global fact of modern India.

Mittal with his very controversial Arcelor bid has put India on the world map very conspicuously. No one can now question the shrewdness and skill of Indians when it comes to business. The fact remains that India had very often faced a prejudice and a backlash from the international community as far as doing business overseas was concerned. Mittal had, however, changed all that once and for all.

The 500 odd crore package to the Vidarbha farmers was a much needed and long awaited. The farmers were simply dropping dead in the region as a sign of protest against the neglect and backwardness of the region. It will, however, be some time before the real impact of the package is felt by the needy of the region.

Spirituality and Superstition

On the blind practices that exists among Indians.

There have often been times when I have looked askance at the lime and chilli concoction hanging on front doors and vehicle dashboards. Today, I know that it wards off the evil eye. There are various symbols in Hindu culture and mythology that stand for auspicious and inauspicious symbols. No Hindu ritual or *pooja* is complete without the *swastika* and the chanting of Om.

Coming to more popular taboos in popular culture, how can one not speak of the evil and bad luck that befalls people when they have a black cat cross their path? Walking under a ladder and opening an umbrella inside the house are again said to bring tremendous bad luck and bad fate. These are, however, borrowed from the West and one really popular Indian superstition would be sneezing when one is leaving for some important work. It is supposed to cause obstacles in the person's work and progress.

A popular superstition among Hindus would be invoking Lord Ganesha before beginning any auspicious task. It is a largely followed practice.

In a lot of drought prone areas, farmers perform the marriage of frogs to please and invoke the rain gods. Whether or not rain follows the ritual remains to be seen, but it certainly provides amusement and laughter for the audience.

The recent Amitabh Bachchan film 'Babul' explores the question of widow remarriage. Though widows are no longer shunned and ostracized in our society, the presence of a widow during a marriage ceremony still happens to be frowned upon.

In Indian marriages it is believed that if a bride's *mehandi* [henna] turns a dark colour, her husband will love her! Let's hope for the bride's sake that this is true!

Spirituality and superstition are, however, two very different issues. While spirituality stands for a direct connection and communion with God, superstitions have more to do with rituals and symbols. While some believe that God resides everywhere, others need an idol to pray to. That the difference between spirituality and superstitions.

Belief in the position & influence of the planets in astrology and the benefits of stones is, however, a part of superstition that does have some scientific base. However, astrology, numerology, and tarot reading are practices that are in vogue nowadays and they offer succour and give direction to the mind during times of trouble and crisis.

Adding an extra letter to your name also seems to be doing wonders for lot of people, especially in showbiz.

However, in smaller towns there are a lot of *tantriks* and quacks who sell bogus powders that are supposed to have miraculous healing powers. Some *tantriks* also advocate human sacrifice to bring better luck. One should be wary of such quacks and not be misled by them. However, there is no denying that these so called spiritual *babas* have power and influence over people leading the country. They often do bizarre *poojas* and *yagyas* in the name of religion. Such people are merely corrupting religion and giving it a bad name and are merely out to make a quick buck! Again, animal sacrifice is another practice that I don't think any religion gives sanction to.

So, if you truly and really want to be on higher spiritual ground, you should connect with nature, help other human beings, eat well and healthy, and keep your surroundings clean. Above all, read the spiritual teachings of the great masters and they will help you attain a higher level of consciousness.

India: A superstar at 60?

A review of Shobhaa De's book on India

This is the name of a new novel penned by none other than the socialite, columnist, and celebrated author, Ms Shobhaa De. Going through a bundle of the latest novels at a local bookstore, what caught my eye was the arresting photograph of Ms De on the cover, and this instantly enticed me to buy her book, notwithstanding her literary skills. The book talks about a shining and sometimes perplexing India at sixtyyears, which is also the same as the biological age of the author. She says that she has been witness to a lot of change within this country; in fact, she has been the change that this country has undergone. She writes, often in her past, she resisted the urge to leave her motherland and go abroad, and she is happy about the decision to stay behind in her country. She watched a lot of her friends leave India for greener pastures abroad and who are today out of sync and not a part of the tremendous progress India has made.

In the book, Ms De discusses whether the benefits modern India is reaping are reaching the lesser mortals of this country or are we in the glow of progress forgetting the marginalized of this country. The IT boom, which has transfigured the skyline of this nation, the growth of infrastructure, the rush to make shining malls and buildings at every corner, the aviation boom, the huge economic growth, and India's new position vis-a-vis the world: Is it here to stay? On the one hand, India is a country caught up in traditions and holding on to age old values and morals. On the other hand, it is a country on the fast track of modernization, where western values are soon catching up.

She talks about the Indians' love affair with big fat Indian weddings, where they go all out of their way to host lavish week-long parties which culminate in a tearful wedding and *bidai*. She ponders whether such an extravaganza and waste of money is justified in a land of hungry starving people. Then she zeroes down on the one topic every Indian refuses to talk about, but is obsessed with—sex! She feels there is not enough statistics and data available in a nation that is very tight-lipped about these things and which still considers sex to be a *gandi baat*. The middle class still thinks that sex is for procreation and not for recreation and this shows why we have such a populous country. That many practice it rampantly without a safeguard also shows why we are breeding and multiplying so fast. She feels that India is a sex starved country and unlike the past where sex was part and parcel of life, today, it is left to furtive coupling on uncomfortable beds, and with tired overworked people preferring the television, to a round of sex in the bedroom, after a long days work.

She writes about how India is a land of contrasts. On the one hand we fancy ourselves as being a peace loving nation that is secular and tolerant, but on the other hand, we have such horrific instances of violence in our country. Right from the past of this country, which has been quite violent, to the latest Godhra carnage and the Nithari killings, everything points to the fact that we have blood on our hands. Bomb blasts, terrorist attacks, communal violence, and daily acts of violence colour our lives. In fact, it would be fair to say that we have become immune to these heinous acts of violence.

Similarly, we have become immune to poverty, dirt, and squalor. We see so much of it around us that we have come to accept it as part and parcel of our existence. We believe that our *karma* has made us what we are, and those who are poor have probably their fate to blame. There is also so much of filth in our towns and cities that we have learnt to live with it. It would be worthwhile to hear and see the shocked expressions of foreign tourists when they encounter ragged and maimed people on the streets or when they come across open sewers, overflowing gutters, and garbage dumps on the roads.

We have also, in our race for supremacy, become quite mammon crazy. Money seems to be the sole aim and end for the younger generation. Almost fifty percent of our population is under thirty-five years of age and this makes our country a very young one. This generation seems to have made money–making its mantra. Money seems to have been demystified and deconstructed, and today, plastic rules! One can also get an easy loan from any friendly bank for cars, home appliances, and electronic gadgets. This easy attitude towards money bewilders the older generation that saved and scrounged all their lives for their old age and for social security. The scenario is very different today. People have no qualms about spending hordes of money on consumer durables and it has indeed become a very consumerist society.

Mayawati may well rule India one day, and it would be fair to say that she has empowered the Dalits of the north and given them a strong identity. When a recent Madhuri Dixit movie titled, 'Aaja Nachle' had words in the lyrics of its song to the effect that a cobbler should not aspire to become a goldsmith, it created a furore in the north, and the director of the film was asked to remove the offensive lyrics and issue an apology, which he quickly did. So, this gives the strong message that the elite do not rule anymore and everyone has equal rights in a country whose constitution guarantees equal opportunities to all. Young men and women are no longer averse to manipulating their caste in order to get admissions in the OBC quota in the colleges of their choice. They feel that it doesn't matter which caste they belong to if they are educated and skilled and have the means to earn a decent livelihood.

Go to any metro and you will find youngsters who are little concerned about which religion or caste their friends belong to. Old family traditions are being replaced by more modern cultures and values. People do not have the time to connect to the extended family and far flung relatives and festivals and births and marriages and deaths often remain restricted to the nuclear family. Things are, however, quite different in smaller towns and cities where the community still congregates during the all important family events.

India rushes to embrace every expatriate success as its own as is in the case of Indra Nooyi, Shyamalan Night, Zubin Mehta, Salman Rushdie, Freddie Mercury, V.S Naipaul, or so many others who have followed. But the fact remains that a few successes on the international scene do not a revolution make. Indian businessmen and policy makers got together at Davos for the economic summit and sang praises of a 'Shining India'. True that India's time under the sun is here, and if we stop being pessimistic about the underside such as poverty, corruption, disease, hunger, malnutrition, and natural disasters, India is certainly glowing and is on its way to a prominent world position.

Women as represented in the Media

Going through the newspapers available locally, one could see that the media was greatly confused about the role of women in society and this was a mere reflection of the mindset of society towards women in general.

Flipping through the local newspaper Hitavada [Nagpur], one could see that it represented women from all sections of society. Although women hardly featured on the front page, except Sonia Gandhi, the second page was generally devoted to celebrity women such as actresses, models, T.V. hosts, and pop singers. These women were all high profile women, and added the much needed glamour factor to an otherwise newzy paper.

The Jessica Lal murder case and the Priyadarshini Mattoo case hogged headlines elsewhere. Both these women had been callously and ruthlessly murdered and justice in both cases was hugely delayed. However, owing to large scale public sympathy for these women, the government machinery seems to have set in action.

Coming to happier grounds, Kiran Desai, daughter of the famed writer Anita Desai, outdid her mother and won a Booker Prize for her second novel 'The Inheritance of Loss' This thirty-five year old unmarried authoress expressed tremendous surprise and gratitude on winning the coveted award, which had eluded her mother many a times.

On the international scene, three business women did India proud by being mentioned in the list of the top fifty most powerful business women. Indira Nooyi, the Indian born head of PepsiCo was top of the list in the US, and the women from India were ICICI bank Deputy Managing Director Chanda Kochar, HSBC India CEO Naina Kidwai, and Bicon head Kiran Mazumdar Shaw.

There were several news items in the city edition of the local paper about women being burnt for dowry and about minors being raped by neighbours, in one case by an inebriated father. Such are the atrocities committed against women that even newlyweds and nubile women are not spared and they become the victims of lustful men.

However, coming to happier grounds, one noticed the sports page full of information about young school girls who had done their schools and teachers proud by winning competitions in sports like swimming, badminton, chess, and basketball. On the national sports page, cricket dominated the news completely, with Sania Mirza being the sole exception in the case of women, and Saina Nehwal in more recent times.

Women's activist Medha Patkar was largely covered with some others like Politburo member Brinda Karat, who had protested against corruption in the Rural Employment Guarantee Programme. She had visited Nagpur and toured Vidharbha where the number of suicides of farmers continued unabated. Irom Chanu Sharmila is another activist from Manipur who has been on a fast unto death for the last six years protesting against the implementation of the Armed Forces Special Powers Act in Manipur.

As Diwali approached, one saw a lot of women's organization in the city organize 'Diwali Queen' competitions. Another organization held a Khoobsoorat 2006 for married women in the age group of twenty and above. Another contest, *Baby Khoobsurat,* had young girls dressed up as older women and parade their stuff on stage. I personally find such competitions for young children highly deplorable. Let's not take away innocence from young children.

Other notable celebrities who were mentioned were reigning actresses Aishwarya Rai, Madhuri Dixit, who was planning a comeback, and Paris Hilton, who is projected as a dumb blonde by the media and who practically does nothing except be paid to attend fashionable dos and been seen out with a new boyfriend every six months. Nicole Kidman's perfect pair of legs was discussed. Oprah Winfrey stated that she felt guilty about being rich, which brought us back to the issue of whether successful women carry the guilt of being successful. Neha Kapoor the Indian beauty queen focused on her international pageant. Madonna planned to adopt an African boy, not to mention the brouhaha that was created over Angelina Jolie and Brad Pitt adopting their Cambodian child Maddox. Malaika Arora Khan was happy to be back on Nach Baliye 2

While Mallika Sherawat declared that what makes a man sexy is what lies between his ears, supermodel Naomi Campbell's temper struck terror again while Monica Bedi got no reprieve from jail following her affair with a don. Ms Universe Riveria was in India on a two-week long tour to promote AIDS awareness.

On the international news page, snippets about them and their representation in the international workforce appeared occasionally. One article talked about how Asian and Black women were amongst the most poorly paid in the UK. They normally got 25% less than their white counterparts being poor role models, working without training and with no growth opportunities.

Queen Elizabeth, who like her elder son, is not a very popular figure in the UK was depicted as a toothless cabbage patch doll by an artist in a British Museum.

There was another gender sensitive article that talked about how women with lower incomes lived fearful lives. They faced financial and emotional insecurity and were seen as a target group for anti-socials making them a highly vulnerable group. One of the most awaited events in the legal arena happened when the judiciary passed the Domestic Violence Act. Here, if a man abused, insulted, or assaulted a woman who was a wife or a live-in partner, he was liable to being imprisoned or being fined Rs.20,000. This law has been hailed by all women's groups and seen as a move to protect the interests of women in society.

Coming to the more marginalized sections of women in society, the pullout page that normally carried articles for glamorous and empowered women did a moving story on the garbage pickers of Mumbai. This workforce of 25,000 odd workers consisted of 80% women, who were mostly Dalits. They were women who were isolated, who had been abandoned or deserted by their families or by unemployed, abusive, and alcoholic husbands. This group has now been trained by a women's organization, and they have been given organisational training with skilled managers and organized into SHG's.

Another article that came was an eye opener had been a cover story in the Sunday TOI about the reigning porn queen in Britain. The article portrayed her very humanely and made us realize that beneath the murky face of pornography, lie young vulnerable women who are driven into this field because of economic reasons and not owing to choice.

Another article which drove home the point about women achievers was about a Bangalore based 23–year-old girl who had bagged a Rupees thirty-six lakhs per annum job as an Investment Analyst in a company that was a branch of the World Bank. This is indeed a new trend in our society where women are moving towards economic independence and self reliance. It also shows that gender is not a drawback as far as achievements are concerned.

In yet another story a defamation suit was filed against Imrana, a rape victim, by her sister in law, which shows that women are often against each other. They are the agencies of a patriarchal system, in many cases, inflicting injustice on other women.

Articles on breast awareness camps and yoga camps for women were many in number in the city edition. Locally, some women took up cudgels against a wine shop and made their men take avow of abstinence. However, some stereotypical advertisements of slimming clinics, jewellery, clothes, and liquor propagated the myth of woman as a sex symbol and the Diva who is fair, slim, immaculately dressed, bejewelled, and an object of desire. The rural woman, the sportsperson, the politician, the activist, and the entrepreneur was lost somewhere within the pages, while these women with perfect faces and figures, semi-clad, and cleavage showing were highlighted on more prominent pages.

The fact that women were desired for their beauty stood out in all the reams of newsprint, with the prettiest woman hogging the show. This message came across quite loudly and clearly.

The IPL 'Tamasha!

The entire country is in grip of IPL fever. The cricket lovers have virtually gone mad as they do not want to move away from the idiot box. The 41-day bonanza like the world cup in which eight teams are vying for the coveted crown involving crores of rupees dominating the world cricket. The celebrities from corporate world and Bollywood have thrown in their lot with the fluctuating fortunes of their respective teams. Will all this help the cause of cricket?

It has been touted as the *baap* of all *tamashas*', `the clash of the titans', and it has turned out to be much more than that! It has ignited the nation's imagination like nothing else before. With eight teams vying for the coveted crown, the forty- one day tourney, in its first phase, has managed to garner all the media - attention. There is much debate speculation in the entire nation about it. Corporate bigwigs and film stars came into the foray to bid for the biggest and the best in the cricketing world. Celebrities like Mukesh Ambani, Vijay Mallaya, Shahrukh Khan and Preity Zinta have thrown in their lot with the fluctuating fortunes of their respective teams. Big names from the cricketing world like Ricky Pointing, Shoaib Akhtar, Adam Gilchrist, Daniel Vettori, Shane Pollock, Mathew Hayden and Kumar Sangakara, have found a place in the various teams that are in the contest. Each team has a brand ambassador and a huge promotional campaign going along with it. Each team has its own uniform and colors.

But the biggest question on everyone's mind is' will the IPL help the cause of cricket Will the IPL help the cause of cricket? Will it help in enhancing the image of cricket in the world, or will it end up just as a marketing gimmick and a much-hyped event with a lot of hoopla surrounding it? The cricketing tourney has also attracted in its wake, a fair amount of controversy. The Maharashtra government found the cheerleaders' performance vulgar, and contemplated banning their presence on the ground. After a lot of hue and cry, the cheerleaders were allowed to perform, but only after they cover up their modesty! The issue did succeed in diverting the focus from the game, though only for some time.

The DLF-sponsored IPL is also to become the highest prize money tournament in domestic cricket anywhere in the world. The total prize money has been touted at Rs. 12 crores, with the winners taking away a cheque of Rs. 4.8 crores, and even the last finishing team taking home Rs. 40 lakh. So the tournament has naturally attracted the best from the cricketing world. A lot of foreign players, when asked by the media if they were enjoying the experience, said that it was beyond their expectations. The size and grandeur of the tournament was beyond anything they had imagined. Add to this a heady mix of glamour, media publicity, and the Indian public's penchant for cricket, and you have a tournament that is huge as a tidal wave! The twenty-twenty league, has also been a blessing for many domestic players who were languishing in anonymity.

The latest controversy to dog IPL is Vijay Mallaya sacking his former CEO, Charu Sharma of the Royal Challengers, for the team's bad performance in the league. Mallaya has also started a blame game by naming Dravid and Charu Sharma for not cooperating with him in the selection of the players. But Dravid and Charu have chosen to maintain a dignified silence, and have blamed poor performance rather than the selection of players for the results.

There have been quite a few stars in the game so far. There has been the old war-horse Saurav Ganguly, who silenced his critics once again by scoring a blistering 91 off just 57 balls in the Knight Riders' match against the Deccan Challengers. Shane Warne too has shown a remarkable performance, delivering his `magic balls' in a tournament considered a graveyard for the bowlers. And now with Shoaib Akhtar- the `Rawalpindi Express'- being given the green signal to play for Knight Riders, the excitement quotient of the game has gone up further?

So, the hype and the hoopla continue, and the Indian public watches mesmerized. This is only the beginning. As the excitement builds up, everyone is keen to know who the winners of the booty will be. All eyes are not only on the technical winners of the game, but also if cricket emerges a winner in the, end!

Afternoon Capers

There is a time in the life of every woman when she finds herself with a lot of free time on hand. Maybe she is facing the empty nest syndrome. Maybe she is a young homemaker who finds her afternoon free. So what exactly does she do during this time?

Elders remember that in the olden days, women used to get together in the afternoons for gossip or to make *papad* or *achar*. But with times changing and with the age of the instant mix, everything has become a lot easier. With upwardly mobile families there are maids in the homes, who help do the household jobs. So it would seem that women, particularly housewives have a lot of free time on their hands. So what does a housewife do in her spare time? How does she kill time?

Go to any household in the afternoons, and you will find women glued to the television. What exactly is it that they are watching? Well, the dreary serials on the idiot box, what else! No one in India would need an introduction to the *'saas- bahu'*, sagas we have on the television. These serials are about the fortunes of joint families, business families, who play in crores. The characters are all regally ^{dressed} and this provides ample fodder for the women at home. Then, the serials are also about the fluctuating fortunes of married couples or young men and women. The characters are all very garishly dressed, and as someone quipped, "'They even go to bed in all their fanfare and paraphernalia".

You would be surprised how the public, mainly, women across

economic strata, lap up these mindless offerings on the television. The serials are not just a means of whiling away the empty hours for them. They religiously follow the fashions and fortunes of the characters, and it has become a point of discussion in their lives. When they meet up with friends, they discuss, the latest styles, saris and jewellery and who died (only in the serial of course), or who made a comeback with plastic surgery. Recently, when the two main leads of a serial were shown as dead, it made headlines on all the news channels. The entire nation was shocked! But then the time- tested tale of *'purnar janma'* (rebirth) resurrected and brought them back on screen, much to the relief of the public. There was this other story of Ekta Kapoor, the mastermind behind Balaji Telefilms, not getting along with '"Tulsi" and the most beloved *'saas'* on television changed faces. But heavy public demand saw her coming back. The actress in question is the dynamic Smriti Irani.

So we have these sagas, which have been running for years at a stretch, and they have made a permanent home in the minds and hearts of all serial watchers, most of whom are women. Never a day passes when these serials are not viewed, and lunch and dinnertime adjusted to accommodate these serials. It is no surprise then, that these television actors and actresses have gained so much fame within the last one decade. Television has become an industry in itself, with its very own set of small screen superstars.

House hold names

Thus Mihir, Tulsi and Parvati became household names, as did Angad, Saloni and many others. These small screen actors enjoy widespread popularity and fame. The television has it own set of takers, with housewives and women from every part of the country, following the travails of theses characters zealously. Rarely is a single day missed, as one never knows what important twist in the story line one might miss out on! The scriptwriters must indeed be a busy lot, what with so many twists and turns to the plot!

So while the producers keep churning out mindless entertainment, the public, which comprises mostly women, keep lapping it up. They are awed by the grandiose sets, the garish jewelry, and gaudy attire of the characters. They love the vamps of the small screen, the most infamous among them being 'Komolika' and among the new breed, 'Sindura'. These negative characters hatched plot after plot to kill off the main characters, but by some divine intervention they survive and come back to take revenge. It would seem as though all of them have nine lives like the proverbial cat!

So these sagas continue, and womenfolk gather in front of the idiot-box to watch the lives of various characters being played out. Maybe it is because their own lives are not so interesting and colourful, that they love to watch the rigmarole on the television. So the mundane lives of crores of women become all the bit more interesting and lively, thanks to these television serials. Each woman has her own opinion about the characters she watches everyday. They are like members of her own family, and sometimes she can even identify herself with the travails of a character. So they give her a kind of emotional catharsis, and keep her addicted to the drama unfolding on the screen. There is nothing 'soapy' about these soap operas, and they keep the woman viewer glued and hooked for years at a stretch!

The Second Sex

The Second Sex' is the name of a famous book by the renowned feminist, Simone De'Beauvoir. The book, which came out in 1949, was a path-breaking **piece of** feminist literature.

She writes about how women from time immemorial have, been given a secondary status. They have been kept confined to the kitchen and the bedroom. For many centuries, women have struggledagainst the stereotype of the passive, docile woman. It was only in the early twentieth century that women struggled for and achieved voting rights.

But the achievements have been few, with women in the, 40's and 50's struggling hard to carve out an identity for themselves. Earlier, it was believed that the role of a woman was to please her husband and cure for the family. Advertisements portrayed a woman as dumb, submissive character, whose role was limited to the home. She was seen primarily as a homemaker, and her role outside home was limited Gradually, the 80's saw the emergence of the independent career woman. Women were finally being accepted in the workplace and even ill positions of authority.

In India, though the position of women has improved dramatically, there is still a very large divide between the rural and the urban woman. Most rural women still live in darkness and ignominy. Young girls in villages are rarely sent to school, and are made to help with the household work. They are often married off at a very young age, since they are considered a burden on the family. In the cities, however, the woman has finally emerged as an entity in her own right. There are many examples of women who have given priority to career. A woman has many roles to play. She is first a daughter, a sister, then a wife, a mother, and also a career woman if she chooses. Society can judge woman very harshly. Her moral character is always under scrutiny, as is her physical beauty. She has to be very careful about her conduct within and outside the family. In a sense, she is always walking a tightrope, which puts a lot of pressure on her. The problems a housewife would face on routine day would be to wake up her children on time, to worry if the milk has been delivered, to pack her children off to school, pack their lunches, worry if the maid will show- up oil time, get the house in order, pick her children up, send them to their tuition classes, get ready to welcome her husband home, prepare dinner, see that the kids do their homework, and finally get everyone ready for bed! An exhusting list Indeed that could intimidate anyone! A working woman's task just gets that much tougher. If she is lucky, she hires a maidservant to look after all these issues, but some of the issues she has to address herself. In addition to these, she has to worry about that appointment with the client, the meeting with the boss, and finally the presentation she has to make before the four o'clock deadline. She also has to get home on time and he there for her children and her husband.

So a working woman definitely finds the going tougher. There are women who on business trips and constantly feel guilty about missing their children's concert or the PTA. They are never at peace. Their minds are constantly in two places at the same time.

To sum it up, a woman is expected to be a paragon of virtue. Her faults are not easily tolerated. The onus falls on the woman, whether it is as an upholder of moral values or of the 'ghar ki izzat'. So women have to tread very carefully on the path of life. They have to chart out their own path and at the same time meet the heavy demands of the society.

A bird's-eye view

When the editor of this asked me to do an article on buildings and builders and on houses and skyscrapers, I was at quite a loss for words. For once, I was at quite a loss for words. For once, I had no ideas flowing out at break-neck speed. I seemed to be suffering from a writer's block. Now what could an arty-farty person like me have to say about concrete and clay! Well, after an initial bout of verbal constipation, my creative juices got to work till finally there was an onslaught of, well, what else—Words! There was a time, not long ago, when one could happily stand on a terrace and gaze far out into the horizon. But with the concrete jungle that our cities are fast growing into, one can hardly stand out on a terrace or balcony without being accused of being a peeping tom or of making eyes at a neighbour's wife. Having lived in Calcutta, where one has to keep one's curtains safely drawn, Nagpur came as a welcome change. No skyscrapers to block one's vision, and one could happily enjoy the beauty of an 'orange' sunrise and sunset, while doing *surya namaskar* on the terrace. If I tired that on my terrace today, I would probably be accused of making obscene gestures at odd hours and of 'exercising' a corrupting influence on the neighbourhood. 'A yogic perversion' indeed! So, no more *surya namaskars* and early morning tea-sessions in the balcony. One has to remain content with the stuffy air of a closed 12 ft by 10 ft room! (So much for my 'Back to Nature' resolutions)

Nagpur, in the year 1991, was, however, yet to catch up on the skyscrapers trend. But the speed and alacrity with which the population of the city seems to be growing and space proportionately diminishing, the day doesn't seem to be far when a skyscraper would be sticking its neck out on the Nagpur horizon.

Builders, however, seem to be making hay while buildings continue to shine in every nook and corner. The metro culture of apartments seems to have taken over smaller cities by storm with people preferring the safe and economical option of flats to independent bungalows.

With the concrete jungle that Nagpur is growing into, one can hardly stand out on a terrace or balcony without being accused of being a 'Peeping Tom ' or of making eyes at a neighbour's wife.

This trend had started rather awkwardly some 10 to12 years ago, when brightly painted pink and yellow buildings had made their appearance on the scene. These monstrositieshad elicited different reactions from various segments of the society. There were those who went to make their abode in this *Kamal* something named buildings and there were those who walked past them, sniggering. Quite a Fountainhead-esque situation! I wonder what Any Rand would have to say and whether she'd send a Howard Roark in our midst to repair prevailing tastes! But a Howard Roark of sorts does seem to have descended on the city eventually, with buildings soon acquiring the look of neat, swanky, modern day buildings!

Plush, white residential complexes with neat straight amenities such as parking lots, constant water supply, and spaces for children's parks began to make their maiden appearances around the city. They promised easy pay by instalment schemes and people swooped upon them in large numbers.

There is, however, a grouse that Nagpur lovers seem to have against building inhabitants. 'Collectivism' seems to breed a kind of indifference, with residents turning a blind eye to peeling paints and chipped faces. There are scores of buildings with an ugly, raw, cemented look. Residents seem to be unmindful of the fact that junk and wet clothes in balconies can make apartments a pathetic eyesore to the neighbours. In their quest for practicality, they seem to have lost all aesthetic sense.

And thus, an appeal to all builders and residents of Nagpur buildings: Please ensure that our city remains green and beautiful. Do not foster an ugly concrete jungle. True, the days of sprawling bungalows and well-tended lawns are on the decline, but we can still ensure a clean and well-planned city. So adios, and I'll meet you for a rendezvous on the moonlit terrace at midnight!

A TRIBUTE TO TEACHERS.

Of gurus and mentors!

Come September and all of us who have frequented the institutions of learning sit back and reminisce about all those individuals who spent their time and energies shaping and moulding our minds and characters.

Listening to Pink Floyd's 'We don't need no education', a song that epitomizes rebellion and bohemianism, one wonders how important those years were that we spent in getting an education. Reality as we see it around us is quite different from the rosy picture painted at schools. Nothing that we have learnt at those hallowed institutions of learning prepares us for the 'real world'. Then, why is it that we spend so many years learning things that we never needed to apply to our daily existence; or then, do we?

As a child, I developed a respect for authority, a respect for all that my teacher symbolized—love, knowledge, and discipline. Having been in and out of several convent and public schools, I learnt to cope in new environments. All through the changing scenario, my teacher remained a constant factor whose love often seemed the easiest to win over. She was my constant companion, the person who knew best. And there was one simple and straight rule to winning her affection—hard work!

Someone once said, 'A little learning is a dangerous thing'. I spent most of my early years at school standing at the corner over the dustbin for being the most talkative girl in class. I would have spent the rest of my life there if it hadn't been for my G.K. teacher in the third standard.

A particularly bad day at class saw us all standing on our benches for a display of incredibly low IQ's! When her anger cooled a bit, our G.K. teacher made us sit down one by one in order of preference (or so we believed). In a class of about 30 odd girls, I was the third or fourth she called out to. I was stunned! She changed the way I looked at myself. Suddenly, every other teacher was looking at me anew; or was it the other way round? Overnight, I had been transformed into a new kid—polite, respectful, and hardworking. It is amazing how one small incident can alter our lives.

As I grew older, I could never forget the value education classes where the nuns drilled 'good morals' into us. We were told not to harbour 'impure thoughts' about the opposite sex! That didn't stop me and my 'gang' from making eyes at the 'macho men' in school uniforms performing stunts on their bicycles outside the school gates.

Over the years, I came to know many members of the infamous species. There was a geography teacher who had travelled the world, twice over. The Hindi teacher made us read Premchand, while she dragged her chair under the swirling fan and dozed off! The biology teacher knew the insides of frogs, cockroaches, and centipedes so well she amazed us. Our French teacher, 'La Dame Sans Merci', made us roll our Rs till we thought our tongues would stick to the roof of our mouths. Our physics, maths, and chemistry teachers inhabited another plane of existence. Unfortunately, our frequencies never matched.

So while science became Greek to me, I turned to the humanities for solace. Life moved on from schools to colleges. Some lessons were learnt within and others outside the halls of learning. Life became a conflict between idealism and reality. Where was one to draw the line?

An M.A. degree was as far as I could go. I felt that I had acquired enough knowledge to walk about with an erudite air! Strangely enough, the first job that came my way was that of a teacher at a primary school. Such are the ironies of life!

It took me some time to get used to being at the wrong end of the classroom. I felt a little ill at ease as the young ones looked at me with adoration writ large over their faces. I minced my words as I realized that everything I said and did had a huge impact on their minds. Young and impressionable they were like sponges soaking in every little detail. Teaching was lot more than merely earning one's bread and butter. I was overwhelmed by the responsibility bestowed upon me. I hoped to do full justice to it.

I said a silent prayer to my teachers. I was back to school and it seemed as though life had come full circle for me. I was a teacher, but deep inside I knew that I would always remain a student—a student in the school of life.

Portrait of a Brother

A character sketch of a sibling who could be anyone's brother.

It's early morning and I'm reading the newspaper and enjoying a cup of warm, delicious tea. Suddenly, my reverie is shattered! A six footer, tall, dark, and er... heavy, man walks into the room; he snatches the paper from my hands, knocks down my cup of tea, and plonks himself on the sofa, legs thrown carelessly on the table! I scream; infuriated and violent images consume my mind. I'm pulling out his hair, throwing a vase over his head and hammering him into pulp! Wishful thinking!

'Betas! Do you remember it's Rakhi today?, my mother's sweet as honey voice interrupts my chain of thoughts. I stifle my demonic urges and remain content with the mental clobbering I gave him.

'Hey, Sis!' Today, you do penance for all the times you have troubled me', says he with a look of pure amusement and devilish glee on his face. 'Me trouble you?' I retorted dumbly, choking over my anger at the injustice of it all. I have realised that despite my brother's interest in the opposite sex, there is one member of the species that he truly detests and that's me! But I am not complaining since the feeling's only mutual.

Friends, let me introduce you to my brother. Dennis the menace Part II:

Twenty years ago, when I was a sweet cherubic angel of five years, a blessed stork delivered a bundle to my house. This bundle of noises that I eyed suspiciously made its home in the crook of my mother's arm. All legs and arms, it cooed innocently and ogled me with large indolent eyes! Thank heavens for the doctor, for he ordered me to keep a safe distance from it as I was suffering from an ear infection. I watched over it from a safe distance while all it did was sleep and blow bubbles into the air!

This bundle of trouble simply grew and grew like Jack's beanstalk before my very eyes. There was a time when I could glare down at him and rap him on the head. I'd have to stand on a chair to do that today, and it would be suicidal to rap someone who pumps iron at a gym everyday! Me and my chair would probably be sent orbiting into space for the rest of our lives! So I have learnt that 'discretion is the better part of valour'.

Our communication remains limited to a bare minimum. Living under the same roof, one develops a thick skin and learns to live by the credo, 'Live and let live'. Normally an older sister is avoided like the plague, unless she is required for money, clothes, or as an accomplice in a minor offence. Arguments explode into long drawn battles. Dare I even talk to his friends or attempt to make polite conversation with them! Female voices on the phone remained another touchy issue that would set the time bomb ticking.

He has reduced me to bankruptcy. There is never a single *naya paisa* in my purse. Our man is either watching a movie, hogging *samosas*, filing fuel in his bike, or devouring chicken at a *dhaba*. And I am sitting in my room and reading a book on 'How to rid your home of pests' (I don't remember the author)!

Come Rakhi and I have to tie the thread that signifies filial ties, love, affection, etc, etc. on his wrist. He zooms into the house, completes the formalities, is thrilled at being the centre of attention, takes money from my Dad, gives it to me, and zooms out of the room again!

Me, the long suffering, sis, helps mom clear up the *pooja* area. I retire to my room to rest my aching limbs. My purse lies empty on the bed. The menace has struck again! I look out of the window and see his disappearing back. I am reminded of a nursery rhyme I learnt as a child at school.

What are girls made of?

Sugar and spice and all that's nice

What are boys made of?

Frogs and snails and puppy dogs' tails

That's what little boys are made of!

FRIENDSHIP

Richard Bach says, 'Joys when extended always increase, and grief when divided is hushed into peace.'

Woe is the man who laughs alone and cries alone and has not a friend in the world to share the sorrows, burdens, and pleasures of life with. The richest man is one who has the goodwill of many friends to stand by him in his hour of need, people who have faith in him and will encourage him in his darkest hour. Our lives are brightened and enriched by the quality of our friendships. We spend our lives chasing material things, little realising that the best things in life come free. Things such as the beauty of a sunset or a rainbow, the happiness of time spent in the company of friends, and the laughter and togetherness of loved ones.

Friendship and love go hand in hand, for we cannot befriend those we do not love. Love is a far more intense and complex emotion, which can at times take on many negative shades. Friendship is a more neutral emotion. We often cannot help failing in love, such a blind overpowering emotion that it is. Friendship is a safer, more platonic feeling which does not get obsessive or clud pour powers of judgement. It involves a certain amount of objectivity where the boundaries between the self and the other are clearly defined. Love on the other hand can become a very threatening emotion where there is a sense of losing oneself in the other.

Linda Goodman talks about soul mates. She believes that there is a special person for each one of us somewhere in this world, and we are destined to meet him or her at some point in time. She talks about teachers, people we meet in our lifetimes, who greatly influence and change our lives. Psychobabble talks about alter age, an image that each one of us carries about our actualised selves. We seek those people who have qualities we admire and would like to possess ourselves. We emulate them, have them as role models, and befriend them. Our egos feel more complete in the presence of such individuals.

Friendship is an expression of our individuality. By finding acceptance among our peer group and friends, we are reassured about ourselves. We make friends with people who are similar to us, those who share our likes and dislikes. Birds of a feather flock together it is said. At the same time, opposites also attract.

Shalini and Pooja were two friends with absolutely nothing in common. Shalini was fat and dark, but gifted with a rare intelligence, whereas Pooja was tall, fair, and beautiful, but the proverbial 'dumb beauty'. They stuck to each other like glue to paper. Each compensated for what the other lacked without feeling threatened by any competition from the other. Shalini helped Pooja get through her exams while Pooja got Shalini the party invitations she'd never have otherwise got on her own. They hung around together, shared secrets, and did odd jobs for one another. Their friendship was never racked by the petty rivalries, jealousies, and back biting that other friendships, especially those between women, go through. In short, they were inseparable. A recent firm 'The Truth About Cats and Dogs' deals with a similar relationship between two women, very different in temperaments and physical appearances, who, however, complicate things by falling in love with the same man. Friends may thus compensate for what we lack or they may complement our own virtues and attributes.

A good friend is indeed a precious possession. But, before we befriend others, we must let go of the 'me' and 'I' and start believing in 'we' and 'us'.

A good friend is a rare treasure to find and is even harder to keep. Friends have been known to keep their bonds alive despite the rigours of time, marriage, childbirth, and careers. Distances have changed people, but not their friendships.

Ravi and Anil were fast friends since childhood. Intelligent and outgoing, they had a lot in common: cricket, movies, and travelling were some of their shared hobbies. Ravi went to the US and struck it big in the fast food business, while Anil stayed on to earn a degree in architecture. Their lives were altered dramatically by the whims of Lady Fortune. However, this did not affect their friendship. Ravi, a successful NRI, still comes and stays at his friend's modest two-room apartment in Mumbai and they reminisce about their good old bachelor days. They relive the moments of their childhood for their families. Their lives and fortunes have changed, but not their friendship.

Friendship knows no barriers of sex, age, religion, nationality, culture, beliefs, or status. Friendship can be struck in the strangest of places with the unlikeliest of people. Co-passengers in trains, teachers and students, the young and old, it leaves no one untouched. There is no reason in the world why an Eskimo and a Red Indian cannot be friends.

Pundits have, over the years, speculated whether a man and a woman can be friends. All time favourite movies like 'When Harry Met Sally' have explored the myths of platonic relationships. A husband and wife can have a successful marriage only if they become friends. A song goes 'How can we be lovers if we can't be friends?' Today, there are programmes on television like 'Ek Duje Ke Liye' which test the compatibility of a couple. The host quizzes the couples about the likes and dislikes of the other. It demonstrates the need for the couple to be friends first. Friendship is a tree that needs to be nurtured carefully. The more we express our love, the more it grows. Through healthy friendships, we fulfil our need to love and to be loved. The art of friendship is also about the art of giving. A thoughtfully chosen gift tells our friends that we care about what they hold close to their hearts. Khalil Gibran dedicates this verse to his friend:

'I care about your happiness

Just as you care about mine

I could not be at peace

If you were not.'

Truly, friendship is all about being a better human being.

Notes On Bollywood!

The KANK Dilemma

'An essay on India's leading director Karan Johar's controversial film, 'Kabhi Alvida Naa Kehna'

Karan Johar's latest blockbuster KANK has landed him in the middle of a controversy which is raging nationwide, occupying the minds of all people young and old, married or on the verge of taking their marital vows. Karan Johar's movies have always been a major hit with audiences in India and around the world. His candy floss vision of life, his sentimentality, his picturesque locales, beautiful men and women, and grandiose sets, not to mention the melodrama and the range of emotions he portrays in his films have seen him emerge as one of the brightest and most commercially successful movie makers of our times. Young people especially identify with his films and feel that he has his finger on the pulse of trends and attitudes of people today. There is a certain degree of sophistication in the range of emotions he portrays be it his film Kabhi Khushi Kabhie Gham, Kuch Kuch Hota Hai, or Kal Ho Na Ho. His movies are typically set in the western world and show big city life with the protagonists being young, trendy 20–30 somethings.

King Khan plays a central role in his films and is probably his muse and inspiration. Kajol is another lucky mascot for his films and always makes a cameo presence in his films if she doesn't happen to be playing the central character. Big B and Jaya Bachchan also figure prominently in his films and he calls Jaya Bachchan a mother-like figure with whom he shares a very close personal equation. His latest presentation Kabhi Alvida Naa Kehna has, however, not once down too well with the masses not being to identify with [the complex story of failed relationships and extra-marital affair. Filmmakers of the yesteryears have tackled this tricky and taboo subject of extra-marital relationships in movies like 'Silsila' where the protagonists played by Big B and the lascivious temptress Rekha plan an elaborate elopement, but ditch their plans at the last minute and run back to their respective spouses. Again, the film 'Arth' explored the guilt and traumas involved in a relationship gone sour due to a man's infidelity. The famous scene of a drunken Shabana Azmi berating and crying over her husband's mistress, played by a strong and sexy Smita Patil, in a party scene will stay embedded in the minds of audiences for a long time. The film 'Masoom' also captures the anguish of a wife when she learns that her husband has sired a child from an illicit relationship and her refusal to accept the child and her final reconciliation with the tragedy of the situation. The young, illegitimate child played by an angelic Jugal Hansraj, who is an innocent victim of this situation, portrays the unfairness of it all where children are often victims caught in the middle of an unhappy conflict.

The movie KANK had two modern couples played by Abhishek Bachchan and Rani Mukherjee and Preity Zinta and Shahrukh Khan, who for various reasons are unhappy with their marriage. Rani has not been able to bear a child and is quite unresponsive to the overtures of her passionate and sexy husband played by Abhishek, who looks absolutely gorgeous in the film. Preity Zinta is shown to be an ambitious and independent career woman who is married to a football coach. Again, their marriage is conflict ridden due to the different values and goals of the couple with Preity Zinta wearing the pants in the relationship. Unfortunately, they have a 5-year-old child who is caught in the middle and torn by the choices this imbalance in the family brings up.

Speaking to a wide range of people from different sections of the society, I realized that there was reluctance among people to discuss these issues. Issues such as live-in relationships, extra-marital affairs and infidelity, be it emotional or physical, were issues most couples were hesitant to talk about. Those who had healthy marriages showed a greater openness to discuss these problems, while others simply pushed the topic under the carpet. Some men were simply uncomfortable to put their relationship under the scanner. Same censored their wives from speaking to us and didn't make bones about it.

Iski Topi Uske Sarr

However, after talking to people I realised that while the common man on the street still believed in the happily–ever-after-kind of love, as one moved up to the higher class, incidences of husbands straying or women having relationships outside marriage seemed to be a little more frequent. Caught between these two classes is the middle class which is too preoccupied with their quest for upward social mobility, greater social acceptance, and, of course, chasing the great economic dream that they simply do not have the time or energy to invest in anything beyond their marriage. Extra-marital marriages seem to be more of an upper class indulgence and luxury, if I may say so. As Shahrukh Khan aptly puts it jokingly in his dialogue in the party scene in KANK that social dos seem to be a place where men get the opportunity to touch other people's wives. The character of Amitabh Bachchan as the skirt chasing widower has also not gone down too well with people, with a news channel giving him a rating of 3 for his portrayal. However, people have come up and told me that they knew men like that who after their wives death coped with their sorrow in various ways. However, I am sure that social censorship would prohibit older people from making absolute fools of themselves. However, one has to realise that Amitabh's character is that of a stinking rich NRI who flaunts a certain kind of lifestyle that not many people can have. Younger people who have gone to see the movie with their older parents have identified with the relationship problems but said that their parents of the older generation simply could not digest it. They kept insisting why the two young couples shown in the film could not adjust to each other.

Pandora's Box

But there is no denying the fact that the movie has kicked up a whole controversy and opened up the proverbial 'Pandora's Box'. It has made couples examine their relationships more closely and ask themselves the big dreaded question—were they to meet someone else, would they walk out on their spouses and family and children? Is it worth breaking a marriage when children are involved? A psychologist in a talk show where Shahrukh Khan, tarot reader Sunita Menon, film director Karan Johar, the CEO of Shaadi.com Mittal, and the celebrated columnist Shobhaa De were the guests being interviewed by the fiery journalist Barkha Dutt attacked the film's director for glorifying infidelity in his marriage. She claimed that several couples had taken the decision to end their marriage based on the message the movie delivered. However, Karan defended his stance by saying that it was just a film and he has not made any strong statements; although in a country where films define and influence popular culture to a very great extent and the majority of the masses are illiterate and just swallow everything shown to them like a sugar pill, it would not be entirely correct to say so. Shahrukh said that though his protagonist is shown to walk out on his child, he would never abandon his son in real life but that is because he has a happy and relatively successful marriage. When his wife Gauri was asked in a chat show what the pressures of being a star wife were and how she would deal with things were her husband to stray, she did not deny that there were insecurities. But she said very bravely that she would pray that she meet someone too, should such a situation arise. I thought that that was a very brave and correct thing to say and a wide and sensible way of coping with the hypothetical situation.

Shaadi Ka Laddoo

A broken marriage is always a very traumatic situation in a society where we are brought up to believe in the happily–ever-after scenario, but one cannot ignore the fact that many people are choosing alternate lifestyles today, especially in the metros, particularly the women. Many women are choosing to lead independent lifestyles where they are not emotionally or financially dependent on a man. They continue to lead normal, healthy lives often having sex outside marriage, sometimes with multiple partners. Many have opted to be single mothers either biologically or with adopted children.

Sushmita Sen, who is termed widely as the 'Original Diva', has an adopted girl child, and she has been famously quoted as saying that this keeps her from marrying for all the wrong reasons. In the Barkha Dutt chat show guests debated that unlike in the west it is still not acceptable in the Indian society to just come in and tell your spouse that have fallen in love with someone else and that you want to walk out of your marriage. The CEO of Shaadi.com argued that unlike the west, the system of arranged marriages was thriving in India and stated that there were no fixed formulae for a successful marriage from all the cases he had seen. When asked by Shobhaa De whether he was married he replied in the negative saying that work and travel kept him too busy to have considered the issue. All this from a sex attractive successful, young bachelor!

On the jacket cover of the CD of the lovely and haunting soundtrack of the film, with the song Mitwa and the title track, Karan Johar questions—'What if you had married for all the wrong reasons such as family pressures or money or you married a friend and down the road you bumped into your soul mate, what would you do? Would you seek personal fulfilment or stay in a marriage that has lost all its charm and lustre?' Disturbing and difficult questions but one we are often faced with. For a woman it is always difficult to walk out of a marriage no matter how bad the marriage may be, and such women are often branded as loose and looked down upon by society. However, it is more acceptable for a man to walk out on his wife and get away with it, unless children are involved. There have been high profile cases of film producer Boney Kapoor walking out on his wife to marry Sridevi, leaving a fat and obese wife of several years to wallow in self pity. Actresses who have access to all the famous men have been known to rock many a marriage. Pertinent to this case being Liz Hurley who hit on the anonymous Arun

Nayyar who conveniently walked out on his wife, Aditya Chopra who is rumoured to have walked out on his childhood sweetheart and wife for the beautiful Rani Mukherjee, and the most notable Ms Sen who has stolen many a man from his wife, the latest being an ad man named Menon who she is to have met on the sets of a shoot where if rumour is to be believed sparks flew between them instantly. She had also appeared very boldly and brazenly on the Simi Garewal chat show with a much married and visibly uncomfortable Vikram Bhatt in tow.

Chaate Pe Taali

There is no age barrier to finding a soul mate in life. For the single and divorced who are in their 30s and 40s, I would like to believe that it's not the end of the road and there is still hope. There was a trend in the West where people married very young while they were still in college and by the time they got to mid life they were breaking apart. This trend seems to be catching on in India with people realising that they have simply grown apart or fallen out of love with their sweethearts. Often, career and lifestyle choices and the demands of a modern lifestyle make couples drift apart. I know of couples who stay in different cities pursuing different careers and stay committed to each other. Above all, I believe great sex is just not enough to keep a couple together. You can make great music together in bed, but when it comes to certain crucial issues in life, the two simply don't see eye to eye. Also, as one grows older, marriage becomes more about mental compatibility and meeting of the minds than about sex alone. That is often the reason couples forgive the partner who strays occasionally or then indulges in harmless flirting sometimes. If the trust and understanding between the couple is good enough, these minor deviations can be ignored. No man is a god and no woman a perfect paragon of virtues. At the end of the day, we are all humans and rounding up, I would say that the film had certainly made people think, touching some, while being totally rejected by others. Commercially, the film seems to have not done too well within the country, but in international markets it seems to have hit the proverbial, **'Pot of Gold'!** The diaspora that is more exposed to alternate lifestyles and knows that the happily-ever-after scenario is merely a myth in the West, which has a very high divorce rate, the situation seems familiar and one they can identify with. However, within the city though gossip and rumour mills work overtime, it would be fair enough to say that a majority of the people are aware of their duties towards their spouses and would think many times over before walking out on them. Women continue to celebrate festivals like *Teej* and *Karva Chauth* and are given the blessing of being *Sada Suhagan*. Marriage continues to be a celebrated institution with familial responsibilities being at the centre of the issue. There is often a stigma attached to the 'D' word, not to mention the trauma involved in the event of it happening.

THE BLOG WARFARE

The latest happening to hit Bollywood is Amitabh Bachchans' offering in the form of a blog.

Amitabh Bachchan has been writing a blog and through this he connects with his fans directly. Despite his eighteen hour daily schedule, he finds time to write his blog. This endears him to his fans even more, and they respond in large numbers. His blogs are very well written. They show that he is the son of a writer, and a highly creative person at that.

Photohraphs and clippings accompany his blog, through which he often takes on his detractors and critics and hits back at them. Whatever Amitabh does, generates a lot of controversy and creates a buzz. This is the case with the blog too. It has led to host of comments and counter blogs. The blog on 'Bigadda' is accompanied by a still from his forthcoming movie, 'Sarkar Raj', and it is an arresting photograph.

Blogging is latest craze to hit Bollywood, and some other actors who have been bitten by this bug are Aamir Khan. Payal Rastogi, Anunag Kashyap and of course Salman Khan. Aamir Khan hit out of both- Amitabh and Shahrukh Khan. He commented that Amitabh overacted in the film' Black which was more like Shakespear's Taming of the Shrew' He felt that nobody would hand over a child, a challenged child at that, to a drunkard; and the scene in whichAmitabh gives a sound beating to the girl was very disturbing. Aamir also hit out at Shahrukh by writing that he had a dog by the name of Shahrukh that was licking his feet while he was relaxing at his home in Panchgani, and that the dog named thus, came with the house. The comments were cheap and there was no reason for the star to make his co-stars look small. He has made the medium a means to take pot shots at his rivals in the industry.

Amitabh , meanwhile, has replied to every negative comment he has faced, including saying a big 'Boo' to Khalid Mohammad who criticized him for his acting skills ill Bhoothnath. Bhoothnath received a lot of mixed reviews, with many critics praising it for its sense of innocence and wide-eyed wonder. Some hotly criticized it for its scenes of'*shraadh*' saying it was a topic unfit for children. Khalid Mohammad, however, made scathing attack on Amitabh, saying that the veteran needed to hone his acting skills and should join the Pune Films and Television Institute.

Payal Rohatgi's blogs were written from the heart. She talks about the embarassment her family faced when she was tagged an 'item girl'. Salman Khan too has taken to blogging seriously, and has written about his upcoming show on television, Dus Ka Dum Shahrukh Khan has, however, stayed away from the blogging game, even though he claims to be very tech-savvy. He seems to be busy making appearances for the IPL tournament and trying to revive the flagging fortunes of his team.

Amitabh made a very touching entry recently when he wrote about the struggle his father faced as a writer, who was often rejected by the publishing world. He writes about how his father rode a bicycle and often fought with publishers when they cheated him of his royalty dues. He even relates an incident where his father braved an earthquake, because he was so engrossed in his work that he took no notice of the mayhem around him.

Junior B has also made an entry where, as always, he praises his father sky high and thanks him for being always there for him through good times and bad. He relates an incident when he was sick or injured and his father left an important function just to be with his son. The entry is real and it once again shows the beautiful bond the father and son share.

The blog is all instant medium to connect with the audience and fans, and you get instant feedback about what you have written. Some fans or readers also hit back with scathing comments, with some getting abusive and calling the stars names. So one must be prepared to take the blows on one's chin with equanimity and retain a dignified silence.

But there is no denying the fact that Amitabh's writing skills show a very superior intellect, and he could give some very talented journos a run for their money. He has taken on journalists such as Shobha De, Yamini Lohia, Harsh Pant for their comments in the media about him. He has chosen to be acerbic and to give it back as good as he gets.

Without doubt, Amitabh's blog is a talking point of the common people, and he has also shown the kindness to write back to hundreds of his fans who have been writing to him. He seems quite undisturbed by the scathing comments made by the media, and defends his family every now and then, especially Aishwarya Rai, his supposedly 'demure' bahu.

Once again Amitabh has proved that he is the master of the situation. Like always, he has emerged the winner hands down, making his critics and detractors look really puny in comparison to his grandeur and stature. The blog, gives us access to the stars like nothing else before, and helps us unravel the enigma behind the facade of stardom. What finally emerges is a very human face behind the starry airs; a face that is real, that hurts. that takes pot shots at others, and one that gives it back as good as it gets!

CONTROVERSIES

Celebrityhood and its baggage!

The latest Aamir Khan controversy surrounding the Narmada Dam Andolan and his open support to Medha Patkar comes as quite a surprise. Activists and other personalities were hotly debating in the media whether it was a good or a bad thing for celebrities to endorse a cause. I believe it is a very good thing for a celebrity to lend his or her name to a cause. It does attract a lot of media attention and coverage, which is a good thing. As for people debating whether Aamir knew enough about the controversy to comment on it is quite ridiculous. To say that they live in a rarified place and are totally removed from reality is also quite ridiculous. His movie 'Fanaa' had been banned from screening in Gujarat. I think a celebrity has the right and freedom to happily endorse any cause he or she believes in without worrying too much about public opinion or criticism. It is a personal choice and they should not be targeted simply because they are celebrities.

Another issue that comes into focus is the latest Feroze Khan controversy, which has led him to being denied entry into Pakistan. Feroze Khan at a public function of the screening of his brother Akbar Khan's movie 'Taj Mahal' commented that he was very proud to be an Indian Muslim, and he said that the Muslims of India were better off than those of Pakistan. I think Feroze Khan was very brave to speak the truth and that too on Pakistani soil and he should be applauded for it. It's certainly not wrong to call a 'spade a spade'. As for Pakistan banning the screening of Indian movies, it reeks of insecurity. Their own film industry is absolutely non-existent and to deny their people the right to entertainment from Bollywood, which is now going global, is downright narrowness and prejudice. But Pakistan has never been known for their maturity and intelligence. General Musharraf may be a very shrewd man who came to India and had the media charmed and eating out of his hands. But the fact remains that India has made gigantic strides in the last few decades and Pakistan needs a lot of catching up to do. But, yes, on the cricket *maidan* they do give our boys a run for their money!

Mahesh Bhatt has encouraged stars from across the border, giving them an opportunity to work in Indian films. A certain actress in question was Meera Ali, who made a lot of noise for all the wrong reasons and disappeared for good. I wonder if anyone ever watched her film. But the kind of statements she made anyone would have thought she was a big star. Recently, she made a statement where she said that her family accused her of *goondagardi* and of not settling down. Earlier, she was reported missing in the Gulf. For those who came in late and missed the action, she acted in a few Hindi films, showed a lot of skin, and smooched on screen and then went back to Pakistan and declared that Hindi movies should be banned in Pakistan. That she is an obnoxious creature is indisputable.

Talking of Mahesh Bhatt, one is reminded of the Parveen Babi episode. I happened to be in Delhi recently where I spent some lonely days all by myself in an apartment and I couldn't help but think about her. She was one of the most gorgeous and glamorous beauties of her time. What happened to her to make her sink to the levels of incoherence and decadence which she did is quite puzzling. That she had a string of failed relationships is without question. A woman needs to be loved and taken care of and any woman will sink into insanity if she is of the sensitive types. Women were never meant to be alone. And to have all her ex-boyfriends and lovers' come before the media and make statements about how she had lost it, was really shameful. It just revealed how ruthless our success hungry society is, that it discards the person who falls back in the race. To see her decomposed body being removed by the police was a tragedy that nobody should have to go through, let alone a famous star. Perhaps, if her friends had stood by her, she would even be alive and smiling today.

A recent story in the Sunday Times of India about the reigning porn queen of the UK, who is of Indian origin, was one of the best stories TOI has carried in recent times. It portrayed the porn queen in a very humane light, which was very touching. One may condemn and criticize such women for their lifestyle choices but the fact that they are human underneath remains.

Good Looking or Good actors??

A prominent talk show host on a television show recently mentioned that if a commercial actor is good looking, then he gets noticed for his physical attributes, and if he is not so good looking, then he gets recognized as a 'good actor' Perhaps this comment was made in jest, but it reveals a bias that exists in Bollywood. Most actors and actresses are noticed for their good looks only. If an actor is good looking, then he or she is not much noticed for his or her acting prowess. Actors like Neha Dhupia and Dino Morea get talked about for their 'good looks' and their physical appeal, whereas actors like Irfan Pathan and Konkona Sharma get talked and written about for their acting skills.

If Aishwarya gets talked about in Dhoom, it's for her amazing sex appeal and her sensual beauty. If Bipasha or Saif get talked about in 'Omkara' or 'Race' then it is for their special 'look' in the film. True, there are some actors like Saif and Tabu, who get noticed in both the categories. Not only do they look good, but they also back their role with some powerhouse performances. Tabu was outstanding in 'Chandni Bar and in 'Namesake' She portrayed roles which difficult for essay. Saif has of late matured as an actor, as has Akshay Kumar the 'Khiladi No. 1 Akshay has quite mastered the action and comedy genre and has delivered some mind-blowing performances, which have catapulted him in the big league. It would be unfair no to mention Amir Khan here as he traverses both the categories. Now that he looks 'choclaty' no more, he has gravitated to the league of good actors, and now that of a good actors, and now that of a good director, with the success of 'Tare Zameen Pe.'

Actors come and go, but it is their look in a certain film which stays in the minds of the audience for a long time. Sridevi was remembered for he chiffon sarees in 'Chandini'. Madhuri will always be remembered as the *'dhak-dhak*, girl and for all the scintillating dance numbers she has performed, be it *'dola-re-dola'* or *'ek-do-teen'* or then the raunchy' *piya ghar aaya'*. The Hritik mania is yet to subside, and his rippling muscular body is what stays in the audience's memory, is his rubber body dance moves ! Shahrukh is known for his sweet-guy-next-door image, and as someone everyone can relate to.

So there are 'good actors' and there are 'good looking actors'. There certainly exist two well demarcated categories in Bollywood. I wonder if you would not be confused about which category Naseeruddin Shah and Shabana Azmi belong to!

Under the Surgeon's Knife

In a field that is ruthless and success driven, it is not rare to see heroines who have gone under the surgeon's knife to enhance their assets.

In an industry where beauty rules the roost, having a perfect figure or flawless features is very important. Many a heroine will stop at nothing to achieve that. Also, a heroine's shelf life is so short that many will postpone marriage, motherhood, and on extreme diets to achieve that one perfect look'

Sushmita is a famous case of a young woman who fell to the demands of fame. the moment she stepped into the limelight, she got her twin assets enhanced. She earlier had a very slim and lithe figure. If you notice her now, she has the fullness of a stone temple figurine. Shilpa Shetty has now acquired world wide popularity and fame thanks to her stint with Big brother in the UK. But before that, she was a struggling B grade actress in Bollywood who had got a nose job done. The results are there for all to see!

Another actress who has got a nose job done is Priyanka Chopra, the beauty queen from small town Bareilly. With her svelte figure and picture perfect face, she is definitely riding high on popularity charts.

No one can forget the irrepressible Rakhi Sawant, who proudly declared on a chat show that she had her twin assets enhanced. And it was all there for everybody to see, as she wore a cream tube top that was a wee bit too revealing! Sheryln Chopra is the latest smalltime heroine who is vying for the sex symbol crown. She has not only got a boob job done, but she has also gone so far as to get her derriere enhanced! It was her gift to her fans, according to what she declared proudly on national television.

So, it looks like the trend is here to stay. In their greed for name, fame, and popularity, women are doing everything to enhance their looks Besides sweating it out in the gym to get that perfectly toned body, they will not think twice before going under the surgeon's knife.

As for men, it's a - desperate attempt to save their hair and stop them from going bald! Many a hero has got a hair transplant done to stop the insigns of ageing. The most prominent among them is, of course, bad boy Salman Khan.

Amitabh Bachchan too struggled with ageing, before he found his footing once again in Bollywood for a successful second innings. Shahrukh Khan has kept ahead of the brat pack by reinventing himself time and again.

So, be it men or women, the film industry makes a narcissus of each actor or actress, who will stop at nothing to maintain their youthful looks and enhance their natural beauty by cosmetic treatments.

A Hit Man!?

Emraan Hashmi is definitely a product of this age. He is a phenomena of today's modern times.

Well, for one he is street smart, smooth talking, savvy, a womanizer, a serial kisser and what not! The success of Emraan Hashmi lies in the fact that a lot of young men and boys can identify with him. He is representative of the morals and values of the new age man, who is quick on his feet, thinks fast, and is not necessarily committed to one woman. He has no qualms about making off with a married woman, as in `Murder', and he in every sense represents the scruples of this generation of young people. Gone are those days when people considered a married woman another man's property, and she was `forbidden territory'.Today's Emraan Hashmis will not think twice before making eyes at a married woman or worse still, luring her to cross her *lakshman rekha'*.

Emraan Hashmi is the blue-eyed boy of the Bhatt camp. He started his career with 'Footpath' in 2003, and then followed the blockbuster `Murder' in 2004. Chocolate, .Aksar. Good Boy Bad Boy, Train, Aawarapan, Zeher, Kalyug, the hit- Aashiq Banaya Apane and the very recent Jannat. have been some of the films he has acted in. If the leading men of yesteryears years were shown to be on the to side of the law, one woman men, moralistic and good, then Emraan Hashmi is the complete opposite of that image of a hero. He is often , if not always , shown to be on the wrong side of the law, treats his women with scant disregard, takes the shortcut to making money, and is arrogant and every bit the anti-hero.

So, just as the heroines of today have replaced the vamps with their sexy item-numbers, so too is this anti- hero here to stay! And it is not strange that a lot of youths today identify with him. Needless to say, he has a large fan following. So, has the antihero replaced the hero? Does the modern day hero have traces of the negative in him, and has he made the villain redundant? Does the audience love the idea of a hero, who i s a rebel, who breaks rules, and lives a risque life on his own terms? Is he an anti-establishment hero who is running from the law and has a precarious existence? Above all, is he an underdog who has no godfathers, and is willing to take all kinds of risks to make it big?

Sometimes he is a hit man, sometimes a crazed lover; sometimes he is an intuitively gifted bookie, who looses his love in search of heaven. Emraan has played all these roles, and many more. A lot of the top actresses have refused to work with him because of his image, but this has not deterred his fans or his supporters in the Bhatt camp who keep believing in him and recasting him in their films. And without fail, this man has delivered. There is no denying the fact that his charisma at the box office certainly works!

The success of 'Aamir'

For those lucky enough to catch the movie Aamir, the success of the film has only reiterated the fact that a small budget film with a new actor can succeed, if the story line is a killer and is backed by a brilliant script.

A film doesn't need big stars to be a hit, nor does it need grandiose sets or mind-boggling costumes or music. A shoestring budget, a TV actor, a realistic situation, gripping drama and some amazing cinematography, was all it took for Aamir to succeed.

Aamir means leader and the film revolves around how a successful. UK returned doctor, gets sucked into the vortex of dirty politics simply because of his religious background. Shown to be a Muslim, the brethren of his community kidnap his family and ask him to commit a crime against his will. The character of Aamir is played by television actor Rajeev Khandelwal, who has portrayed it exceptionally well. The dialogues in the movie are minimal. The camera focuses on the tense faces of its central characters and catches the scenes of the decrepit and run-down localities and ordinary people living there, as it takes you through narrow by lanes of the metropolis Mumbai

There is no heroine in the film and hence no romantic angle. The story ends in a dramatic climax within two hours. But the movie keeps you on the edge of the seat, and you cannot but sympathize with the protagonist, who is a man with a promising future, caught in the dark world of religious politics and terrorism. The movie has been produced by Anuraag Kashyap, and is a UTV production directed by Gupta.

Rajeev Khandelwal has portrayed the character brilliantly. He looks intriguingly handsome as the suit clad, suave, London returned doctor, who is at once baffled and heartbroken by the news of his family's kidnapping. His helplessness and frustration at being played around like a pawn in a chess game is apparent and palpable. His only concern throughout the film is for his family, but towards the climax of the film he emerges a hero and sacrifices his own life to save the lives of hundreds of innocent people. This truly makes him an `Aamir,[savior] not just for his own community, as the villains of the film wanted him to be, but also for humanity in general. Your heart bleeds for this young promising life brought to an inglorious end by the misdeeds of some misguided members of his community. The movie should certainly get some critics awards for its brilliant storyline, and is certainly worth a dekho

Code of Conduct at the work place

At the beginning of one's career, when one is not backed by experience, one wonders about the nature of work to he undertaken. One must remember, that no work is small or menial or degrading. During your learning years, one must imbibe everything. The mantra should be talk less and observe more. No matter how small a task may seem, one must apply oneself to it with all sincerity. Superiors and seniors should be respected and colleagues given heed to.

One must be a rock-star at work! This means that all tasks should be undertaken with enthusiasm. .Your work should be something you enjoy. You should report to office on time and leave at the affixed time. Unpunctuality and absenteeism create a very bad impression and should be avoided at all costs.

Be the eternal optimist. Don't let small setbacks hurt you. You should be able to bounce back from every adversity. Value people, be an original, laugh and have fun. Too many of us are afraid to be ourselves, so we give up our dreams and follow the crowd.

They will also introduce you to a new set of possibilities. Doors your never knew existed will begin to open. You must always try to get what you want, while loving what you have.

Listen twice as much as you speak. Learn to say no. Remember that being a leader is not about being liked or being popular. Real leadership is not about power, status or prestige. It is about responsibility.

It is also important to have good manners. They are a stepping stone to being a good human being. So, be wildly enthusiastic, energetic and madly alive. It is never too late to become the person you have always dreamt of being.

Life is too short to be miserable. Remember at the end of the day, the billionaire gets buried next to the sweeper. We all end up as dust. So he nice to people and have fun. Make your workplace a place you look forward to going, everyday.

'Pages from my blog'

To be or not to be

I have always been the real-life Hamlet, taking eons to arrive at any decision. I believe that there are two sides to every story as there are two sides to a coin. I am always in the eternal dilemma.... To be or not to be.......

Hi folks!

It feels great to be here as I am a novice in the world of blogging. It is nice to be able to give vent to your feelings and express oneself so openly. I have read quite a few blogs and am amazed at the quality of work. Blogging has spawned its own share of celebrities and personalities, some of who are famous and others relatively unknown. It's amazing and mindboggling to see the talent on display. It would be fair to say that with technology reaching the standards it has, push button publishing has taken creativity to unparalleled heights.

Hopefully, I should be around longer to read more, write more, and make new friends.

Ciao!

A new day!

Hi,

So, now that I am officially a blogger, let me begin by telling you something about myself. I am a highly confused, single woman, who may not hold the view she so thought dear yesterday. My perspective on life changes on a daily basis. Yeah, I am confused as hell! True, I was not always like this, but circumstances and experiences have made me this way.

I used to think I was a rather straightened-out woman, but the more I think about the past, the more confused I become. Yes, I had beliefs like everyone else—strong, unshakeable beliefs—but life's experiences changed all that. And frankly, the farther u travel, the less you really know!

Yeah, this is a Beatles song, and I truly believe in it.

There was a time when my world was small, but I still believed I owned it. That was when I had a man in my life. Now I don't, and this makes me feel lost. You may think I am a weak person, but believe me I am made of strong stuff, but men have confused me. I guess I will never figure them out either.

Life is a roller coaster ride, to use a cliché, but indeed it has been for me. And, I invariably land with a thump. Has it made me cynical? Has it jaded me? Not really. I go on with expanded horizons, but a slightly confused state of mind. Am I difficult to understand? I guess I will never know.

Hi,

I definitely think that fact is stranger than fiction. You don't agree? Well, pause to think again. I truly think that art borrows from reality and not the other way round. All that we see around us, our movies, and serials are all inspired by some event in real life. Art wouldn't exist if it were not for reality. Every writer of a book or a director of a movie has, to some extent, been inspired by events borrowed from real life.

Every creation of art has the creator's personality as its background. It is shaped by a creator's imagination which must again be coloured by events in an artist's life. He must have at some point experienced what he wishes to give credence to or seen it even if in his dreams. Dreams, again, are shaped by events stored in our subconscious mind.

Writing is therapeutic and cathartic as we give vent to our feelings, emotions, and visions. They get the shape of reality in our creations. We script our own world, our own reality. Reality is not out there, it is in our minds. The physical world is just an illusion.

The man in the suit!

It was early in the year! The cold was still in the air. Her levels of frustration had reached peak level. She had applied for a job at several places, but had been turned down. She was at her wit's end. Here she was qualified with significant experience behind her. Couldn't she get a decent job? Finally, when her patience had reached its nadir, she received a letter in the post. It was about a job she had applied for in a premier management and teaching institute at Delhi. Luckily, the response had been positive. They were offering her a position with their soon to be launched magazine, as an assistant editor. She was thrilled. They were paying as good as any competition, and she immediately took up the offer! She was asked to join within a week's time.

She packed her bags and bought her tickets. Shortly, she was in the capital and walking down the road to the institute. It was one of the premier institutes of India and had glamorous, swanky campuses and offices! She paused at the entrance taking in the atmosphere, the young students, the corporate guys in their expensive cars, and the pretty women of Delhi. She entered the office intimidated by what she saw. She checked in at the reception and waited for someone to call her.

A young man came out shortly. He was tall, lanky, and had a clean shaven head. So this is how they wear their hair around here, she thought. She was intrigued by his dynamic personality and found herself tongue tied as he addressed her. He asked her to wait for a few minutes as he was in a meeting and said he would meet her shortly. When he had gone, she turned to ask the girl at the reception who he was. The girl answered that he was their young CEO and was responsible for all new recruitments.

Shortly, she found herself seated opposite him in his cabin. He was charming, funny, welcoming, and made her feel at ease immediately. As she soon found out, he was Oxford educated and was heading the publishing section at the institute. He was barely

25, but shouldered immense responsibilities, travelling across the globe to handle other offices of the institute. He was the new kid on the block, the maverick, and the others referred to him in whispered tones as the genius!

She got a desk in the corner with a brand new PC to work on. As the days passed, she wrote some articles, interviewed people, but she constantly found her mind occupied by her new boss, and couldn't help stealing a glance in his direction as he sat grim faced, his face a mask of concentration, in his glass cabin across the room.

Days passed without any significant happenings. She continued to write stories which more often than not got rejected by the editor. He was a difficult man to please. Sometimes, she would take the articles to his cabin for his approval. He was kind, gentle, and listened to her views with approval and appreciation. This greatly encouraged and gladdened her heart. Sometimes, she would find him looking in her direction through his hooded eyes and she would blush a deep pink and bury herself in her notes. Sometimes, when they were exchanging notes, he would offer her a drink and she would accept it gladly. She admired the suits he wore to office daily, taking in the details, his aquiline nose, the glasses on them, the neat fold of his pleated trousers, the broad chest!

One afternoon, she saw him talking to the secretary and realized that he was going for one of his official tours. He was flying to New York for a week. She tried to focus on her work and knew that she would miss his absence. That afternoon, the disgruntled editor called her to his office. He reprimanded her about some article he had asked her to write and she had refused, saying it was beyond her scope of understanding and subject. The editor lost his temper and fired her without warning. She rushed out of the office a mess of tears! She was too proud to make a case for herself and knew that the editor had for some reason taken a dislike to her and was looking for the first opportunity to fire her.

Even the kind boss was not in his office to hear her point of view and perhaps support her. She tried calling him desperately, but she was informed that he was out of the country by now.

She moved her things out of the office. She knew she had no choice but to go back to her hometown. She stayed on for a few more days trying for other jobs, but nothing worked. She waited for the young man to come back, but she never saw him again. She tried calling him up, but he was generally busy in a meeting. She knew she would probably never see him again and she returned with a hole in the heart and some bittersweet memories.

Thursday, February 4, 2010

An affair to remember

She sat in the coffee shop, her back against the wall, facing the crowded room. Youngsters strolled in and out of the cafe. She saw him across the room, sitting on the far corner having a coffee with a pretty young thing. She felt embarrassed and discomfited. She felt the blood rush to her cheeks. She didn't want to remember the time she had spent with him. It had been a short, passionate affair. He was younger than her by a good many years. He was a young, strapping, tall, lad, and she had been smitten by him the moment she had laid eyes on him. She looked for the stud in his ear, the short stubble and the cropped hair. It was all there! He was an engineering student who lived in a flat with a friend. They became friends, and often when the flat was empty, they would spend some stolen moments in each other's arms. The sex was hurried, passionate, and intense. He was a young lover and made her feel wanted and loved. She was not the least conscious of being older, and their compatibility was spontaneous. Often, she would walk into the flat when he was working out in the evenings. She could see the rippling muscles of his back and the beads of sweat on his forehead. His physicality was overpowering and he was a large man for someone so young. But there was a sweetness in his face which could not disguise his age, despite all the false bravado he put on.

But she was always afraid of the younger women around him. He was a handsome man and naturally attracted a lot of feminine attention. She agonised over who he would meet in college and the girl friends in the canteen and she began to feel insecure. She jumped out of her skin every time a friend called up and someone crossed them. Also, he was a little averse to be seen publically with her. He didn't know how she would fit into his younger gang! And she was more than aware of his discomfort.

Today, she was meeting him after a year. He had finished his studies and gone back to his hometown. She tried to catch his eye to see any sign of emotion. But there was none. He continued to laugh and joke with the nubile young woman beside him. He has terrible choice in women, she thought. Here I am, a sexy older woman, and what could he probably see in those gawky teenagers.

But she realised how futile it all was. Mentally, there was a big chasm between them, and a big gap of years and experience separated them. He was a young man after all. And younger folks have looser morals these days. They don't understand the word commitment. It's like wherever I lay my hat that's my home!

Saturday, January 23, 2010

Jaipur Literary Festival

I just got back after attending two days of the Jaipur Literary festival. Missed out on meeting some of the other members from Caferati or just overlooked them since there was such a crush of people. It was a truly international festival of food, music, art, theatre, and, of course. books. There were the likes of internationally acclaimed writers like William Darymple, Geff Dwyer, Esther Freud, Ali Sethi, Amit Chaudhuri, Amitava Kumar, and Vikram Chandra taking part in intellectual discussions and promoting their books. There was Shabana Azmi introducing her mother Shaukat Ali's writings published by Zubaan, Girish Karnad, and Om Puri with his wife Nandita promoting their book an 'Unlikely Hero'. Despite the controversy surrounding the book and the ugly public spat between the husband and wife, I found the book honest and truly revealing of the man and the actor Om Puri and his wife has done a commendable job of it.

Barkha Dutt was moderating a session on 'Can books survive the Internet'. I found her loud, brash, and opinionated, but then, maybe as a journalist u need to be one! Tina Brown, the renowned American journalist, was there, promoting her newly launched website, 'The Ugly Beast'. She was a picture of professionalism that American journalists are known for. Gulzar was read out his neglected poetry, as he called it with an English translation by the writer Pavan Verma. Gulzar is a man of deep sensibilities and his poetry is languid, reminding you of a bygone time when time stood still. He makes astute observations and comments on everyday things like the fan, a bird in his room, a sunbeam filtering through his window, the rain, and many more everyday things. The man's genius is unsurpassable as are his poetic sensibilities. The English translations by Pavan were just as good or nearly so! There was a discussion of Dalit literature, which is gaining relevance in these times of equality. The festival was truly democratic in this sense. Vasundhara Raje, the chief minister of Rajashthan, made a quiet entry and stood in the corner of the crowded room without any fan fare or a coterie following her. Bina Ramani and other celebrities went away almost unobserved. The spirit of the individual was on display and each human being was special. It was a beautiful atmosphere to soak in the warm Jaipur winter with *masala* tea being poured by a young man dressed in traditional Rajasthani attire in an earthen mug [Kulhad].The food was delicious as was the wine and beer being served on the house. There was traditional Rajashtani cuisine such as *dal bati* and *gajar ka halwa*, as was there pasta and chicken in white gravy for the more international taste buds!

It was a truly awesome experience!

Random Musings!

I have been looking up Tina Brown's website, 'The Daily Beast' and enjoying reading comments on various issues. There was a write up on Susan Boyle, the British reality show winner who was all over the news of late. She was the winner of a singing talent show and the attention of the entire world hovered over her for some time. She is a fairly dowdy looking woman in her 50's, and while one did appreciate her singing talent, one could not but feel ambivalent about the way she looked! She is a clumsy dresser, most unattractive to say the least and as she confessed on T.V., someone who had never been kissed. She lived alone in the suburbs of the UK, and that she had obviously lived a life of anonymity and neglect is anyone's guess. But post the reality show, the media was all over the place trying to peep into her life, and for a short while she enjoyed the spotlight and was the darling of the media!

In a glamour driven world, this was an instance of a kind where someone old and ugly and almost invisible was being lauded by everyone. In this age of superwomen, achievers, and glamour dolls with hourglass figures, this woman suddenly had the media by the horns. I think it brought out issues like 'is beauty skin deep?', and 'can we ever look beyond the physicality of an individual to appreciate what lies within them?' She brought the focus on a lot of ordinary women who go unnoticed and are almost invisible all their lives! Something to think about!

I also recently read a comment about how reviewers in the UK hate to critique Salman Rushdie's works because even if they might find it bad, they cannot say so because the author has such a formidable reputation in the literary world. This brought me back to a panel discussion we had at the JLF, which discussed the importance and the role of reviews of books by fellow authors and whether they were genuine and had any effect on the sale of the book or its fate in the market! I personally am suspicious about these reviewers and prefer to use my own discretion while buying a book.

Talking about authors and their books, one wonders why a Chetan Bhagat or then a Shobhaa De invites so much criticism from the literary pundits. True, these authors are no literary craftsmen, that is not to take away from their writing skills. But they write in a way that the layman connects with them instantly. They write about a reality that a majority of people can identify with and that alone explains the commercial success of their books. As Chetan Bhagat explains, an Infosys cannot be a Google, but that doesn't in anyway suggest that Infosys is a crap company! I am personally a big fan of Ms De and follow her blog relentlessly, and as for Chetan Bhagat, I think that he is a good storyteller and there is a simplicity and charm in his writings which is appealing especially to the youth. And it is a fact that he is a huge youth icon today.

So much and much more occupying my mind. I will share some more of my musings with you shortly. Till then, take care and see you around!

Saturday, December 19, 2009

Sally and Joe!

They were like Siamese twins, always hanging out together. Ever since they left college, rather dropped out, they were like twins joined at the hip! Joe had rented an old yellow caravan, and they set out to explore Europe on a meagre budget. Sally danced at nightclubs, while Joe played the guitar and sold his short stories to the local newspapers for a pittance. He wanted to be a writer and knew that a little bit of worldly experience would take him a long way. Sally wanted to be a ballet dancer, but had no formal training as her poor father could not afford it. So, she concentrated on losing weight to become a model. She wanted to go places, Paris, New York, and rub shoulders with all those wonderful glamorous people one saw in glossy magazines! They set out in search of their destiny, leaving their small obscure town in Germany, sometimes washing dirty dishes and mowing lawns to make ends meet.

They were madly in love with each other and that was their sustenance. They had no clue what promises the future held out for them, but they were willing to put everything at stake to give it a shot! They travelled the length of Europe, meeting vagabonds, tourists, rich restaurant owners, corrupt editors, and lecherous men, sometimes women.

One evening while Sally was dancing at a night club, the fat, rich owner called Sally to his table. It was Saturday night, the music was playing loud, drinks were being passed around, and a garrulous crowd was in the club. The owner introduced Sally to a movie director from America. He promised to make Sally a star, but she would have to join him within a fortnight since he was sailing back in his yacht to the UK, from where he would catch a plane to Hollywood. Sally was confused; she didn't want to leave Joe behind, but the man wouldn't take anyone else with him. She was caught between pursuing her dreams and her unflinching wide-eyed love for Joe!

That night, while Joe slept peacefully under the stars, she took all the money they had saved and quickly scribbled him a note and slipped out in the dead of the night. In the morning, when Joe woke up, he saw the note in which Sally had scribbled hastily, 'I will come back to you the day I become a star! Joe knew that Sally had made up her mind and he would never be able to get her back. Although broken hearted, he lifted his spirits and went back to his old town. His heart had a scar on it, but the wound had given him a depth and a new perspective of life, and he knew he would be a great writer one day!

Two young people, two different worlds, but they toiled and one day realized their dreams, though separately. Their love was the scapegoat, their fates and destinies took them apart, and though they were successful, innocence was sacrificed and their promises of an undying love turned out to be a farce!

Wednesday, December 9, 2009

Tiger and his sins!

I am at once dismayed and disappointed with the media attention on the life and times of Tiger Woods. One day this man is declared to be God and the very next day he is being pulled down to the ground because of his personal affairs, which have been made very public. It all started with a crash in which Tiger reportedly banged his car against a fire hydrant and a tree and drove off the kerb after being pursued by his wife with a golf club after his affairs came to light. He was reportedly having an affair with a night club hostess and his wife seemed to have found out.

Ever since then, the media has gone nuts, digging out the umpteen women he is supposed to have slept with, and his private life is very much in the public domain now. For a man at the very top of his career, this fall and public scrutiny of his personal life has indeed been shocking and humiliating. He has been made the butt of jokes and his standing has spiralled downwards in a jiffy. From being idolised and held as a perfect example of a sportsman having a squeaky clean image, his reputation has taken a beating and been dragged to the mud. Every day, the papers are full of salacious reports about the sexcapades he is reported to have had; a British doctor has also declared him to be sex crazy.

A site which had him lionised as God has shut down and many brands which he had so far endorsed are said to be having second thoughts about using him as the brand ambassador. Many media pundits have been making comments about him going public with his transgressions on public chat shows such as Oprah or David Letterman. I for one have never been able to understand the alacrity with which the media can build up someone's image in the public's eye and then tear it down one fine day! Having a marriage put under scrutiny is difficult enough and especially so when one is a public figure and a celebrity. Tiger has been married to his wife of 5 years Elin, a model, and has a year old son from her.

A sportsman of his calibre with a foreboding reputation in the sporting world can have his standing and image and also his career destroyed in a minute because of his affairs and his transgressions. He claimed on his website that he had let down his family and asked for the media to respect his privacy and let his personal sins be private. But far from that, his affairs have become the fancy of the media with detailed reports and cell phone conversations between him and his mistresses. Made public are the number of sexual encounters he has had with them and also those he had when his wife was pregnant. His mistresses have given details about their encounters, some saying he was a lousy lover and others claiming that he was a dominating lover who was also very well endowed, considering he is a sportsman and knew what he was doing.

All said and done, it's a sad state of 'affairs' and a fall from grace of one of the most loved, respected, and successful sports personalities of America. His popularity was such that it made him a much loved and admired figure not just in the USA but across the world. It's sad to see a man of reputation being pulled to the ground in this sordid fashion. May God give him and his family peace in these trying times and may he emerge stronger from the ordeal.

Thoughts at midnight!

I had to write. It was midnight and a million thoughts were cruising through my mind. I couldn't sleep. I tossed and turned. I groped in the darkness into my purse and pulled out my notepad and pen. I was on the top berth of a train hurtling towards Delhi. I felt old. Thoughts and emotions weighed heavily on my mind. A marriage had come to an end. A decade of a trying, difficult, and eventful relationship was unravelling. Life had taken us down different paths. Our choices and needs had torn us apart. Our love had been turbulent. We thrived on conflict. But finally that had to end. And there was a deafening silence. It was over. But funnily, I wasn't feeling fragmented or broken. I felt strangely complete. The love had made me grow up. There had been lessons learnt and personal growth. And the love was not dead. It was inside me; only life had moved on. A new beginning, a new turn, a new relationship, and new challenges. A sense of maturity and a life ahead. I felt a hundred years old. Would I survive the transition? I read a poem about maternal love. It made me uncomfortable. I hadn't had the opportunity to be a mother. The thought daunted me. So many more milestones. So much behind, so much yet to come. As life unfolds, we learn some lessons in retrospect, yet we feel completely unprepared for the challenges ahead. I had to write. It connected me to reality, it put things in perspective. Now I understand why some people say they write because they had a compulsion to write. Frankly, it was the only thing I knew. It was midnight; I had to write.

Why do fools fall in love?

Rage overtook her. Her body trembled. She thought about when she had first met him. Charming, attractive, and devilishly handsome, he stood out in a crowd. She had felt a thrill of excitement as he had walked up to her. They became friends fast and spent time in each other's company. Days became weeks and weeks, months. Time flew in his company. There was, however, one problem. He was a married man. He had not hidden the fact from her. He had a wife and a child. She kept hoping against hopes that he would leave them for her. She kept waiting for that fight which would eventually break up his home. After all, he was having an affair. Surely his wife would find out. But she kept waiting. The defining moment never happened. At the end of every feverish and passionate time spent in her arms, he would go back home to his wife and child. And she would go back to her lonely bed and lie awake all night, tossing and turning.

He was a sexually dominating man and though he focused solely on his pleasure, she wasn't complaining. She felt a sense of belonging and fulfilment just being in his arms and being made love to. She treasured the precious moments spent together. She often visualised him at home with his family, in the cosy confines of his opulent home, quietly playing the man of the house. His family needed him and he could never abandon them; that was his usual refrain. And she would never make an issue. She felt that perhaps her love would win him over. But this evening was turbulent.

The skies were dark and there was a strong wind blowing. He had cruelly and abruptly called the relationship off. He told her he didn't need her any more. He had other priorities and he was tired of the relationship. She felt shattered and abandoned. Her heart felt like it had broken into a thousand pieces. She didn't know what to do, where to go. She had no one to turn to, no one she could confide in. She knew she had been in the wrong, abandoning all logic and reason to love a man who was already committed. But love knows no rules. When it hits you, you are caught unawares.

She took out her coat and the car keys. She felt blinded with rage and fury. He had used her and thrown her aside like a piece of old cloth. She drove blindly on the streets. She thought she would go to his house, confront him, and reveal all in front of his wife. She would make a scene. She would cry and implore him to come back to her. Maybe she would shatter the glass of his brand new red car. All kinds of revenge fantasies played out in her mind. She finally realised the futility of her actions. She would only succeed in making a fool of herself. He would remain cold and unmoved. He had a heart of stone and she had loved him. She said a silent prayer and forgave him. Tomorrow was another day and she would survive. She went back to the privacy of her home to lick her wounds. She wanted to cry and howl, but there was a deafening silence. It only signified the end. The end of a relationship and a broken heart.

Scent of a woman!

I was sitting at a local coffee shop and the thin skinny woman sitting at the adjoining table reminded me of a writer I loved and admired, Shobhaa De. She was skinny and sharp featured, just like the abovementioned woman. Though I don't like to admit it, Ms De has been an inspiration during my formative years as a writer. I closely followed every little 'byte' on her, what she wore, the parties she attended, the people she socialised with, and, of course, what she wrote! The descriptions of sex in her novels were fresh, raunchy, and wholesome'. *Paisa vasool*, 'to use her lingo. Her earlier novels were quite naturally a throwback to her earlier 'risqué' lifestyle, and I admired the strength and independence of a fiercely bold and independent woman.

Coming back to some more contemporary women, I have secretly envied the slim bodies of a 'size zero' Kareena, Aishwarya, or Queenie Dhody, the socialite, the curvaceous Shilpa Shetty, who are all high maintenance women. The sleek models on the ramp such as Jesse Randhawa, Alicia Raut, Nina Manuel, Carol Garcias, Sheetal Malhar, Vidhisha Pavate, Fleur Xavier, Noyonika Chatterjee, or even designers like Ritu Beri, Rina Dhaka, and Malini Ramani, who would give any model a run for her money! I have always had weighty issues and was never quite comfortable with my body. As a teenager and then as a young adult, I struggled with a yo-yo body weight and had serious body image issues. I would be an anorexic one week, eat like a bulimic the next, exercise like a mad woman the next, never quite knowing where to strike the balance. I went through periods of emotional turmoil and stress, and at every stage, food became my crutch. Like most young women, I abused my body, put on weight, went into depression, and it was an endless cycle. Now in my thirties, my weight issues are far from being resolved though I am more at peace with my body type and image and no longer go into a frenzy every time the scales show a few kilos more.

With experience that age gives you, one develops an inner sanctum of peace and stability. Life is not so much about physical appearances and what lies beneath the surface matters more. A preoccupation with the outer shifts to a dependence on the inner.

As these thoughts drifted across my mind, I noticed another pretty thing on another table with attractive bangles on her wrist. I have always been obsessive about fashion, having a fascination for clothes, jewellery, shoes, bags, and the works. Whatever meagre earnings I earned I spent on collecting every bit of new 'trinket' in the market. My earnings never gave me the luxury of indulging in 'haute couture' or designer wear, and I happily spent on 'street fashion' which had a style and character of its own. I enjoyed putting on an ensemble together with mix and match ingenuity. The famous Janpath of Delhi, Fashion Street of Mumbai, and flea markets of Goa were my favourite haunts.

As these thoughts flitted across my mind, I realised my coffee was over and the tables around me were empty. I realised it was time to move on. I paid the bill and walked out into the sunlight. There was a gentle breeze blowing and it felt good to be alive.

Friday, October 9, 2009

The Austerity Drive

First, it was about the Tharoors and Krishnas inhabiting 5-star accommodations. Then, they got at other ministers who spent crores of public money on foreign travel and also by travelling business class on international flights. The government advised all government officials to follow austerity measures and start travelling economy class. Then the infamous Mr. Shashi Tharoor, writer, parliamentarian, ex-ran for UN secretary general, made his most unfortunate remark. He called the economy class cattle class, thus hurting the sentiments of millions of Indians. And all this was due to a tweet he tweeted on Twitter, the new age social networking site, proving what an uber cool, net savvy, new age politician he is. Then came the hundreds of comments deriding his remark and as a prominent columnist put it, she said he works so hard to look pretty that he complains about his work pressures, including travelling economy class like the common junta! Then came the clarification that he was referring to the way the aircraft people herd in the people in the economy class. But it was too late by then. The damage to the Indian psyche had already been done.

So now the Indian government is on an all out austerity drive. They have even asked INC India to reduce the salaries of the CEOs. This is in the right spirit considering the exorbitant salaries some of them demand. All these measures send in the right feelers to society which already is caught in a divide between the haves and the have-nots. The chasm between the rich and the poor just keeps growing larger. As a lot of economists and social scientists have predicted, it could lead to a serious conflict between the two and serious social upheaval.

As an example, I would like to cite the case of businessmen playing cards during Diwali. Some of them play such high stakes and money just flows like water. It is an almost obscene and frightening comment on our society that while on the one hand farmers in the neighbouring Vidharbha continue to commit suicides, the elite of the society should amass and waste such precious wealth which could be used for better and nobler purposes.

I think it's time for all of us to follow serious austerity measures. The lifestyle of the average Indian has become so exotic with foreign holidays, shopping at malls, trips to expensive spas and resorts, and international schooling for the kids and designer homes. On the other hand, in sharp contrast, we see stark poverty and families struggling to make ends meet. This struggle sometimes leads to crime and people resorting to anti-social means to earn their livelihood.

I think it's time we stepped out of our ACs and designer lifestyles to spare a thought for the less privileged. I have always believed that the people of this country have become immune to poverty. Let's change that and pledge to work for the general uplift of society and the poor and less fortunate.

The Ranji Trophy Player

There was a young lovely woman who went for long walks by herself in the evenings. The sun would have set and the cool breeze of the pleasant evening lulled her senses to calmness. As she walked down the road, she could see the silhouette of the trees against the rising moon in the sky. She walked totally absorbed in her thoughts quite oblivious of the vehicles and people passing her by. She recognised the regular walkers and acknowledged their greetings with a smile and nod of her head as they crossed her. People seemed too caught in their own lives to give her more than a curious look.

One evening she saw a young man jogging down the same road. He was tall, well built, and handsome. He often gave her a look as he sped past her. She noticed him too, but was too shy to acknowledge him. Then, one evening, he gave her a shy tentative smile and stopped to talk to her. They exchanged pleasantries and asked each other's name. He told her that he was a Ranji Trophy cricketer and worked at the local branch of a national bank. He came from a simple working class background. He had lost his father a few years ago and was the man in the family looking after his mother and younger brother. He asked her how she spent her evenings and she replied that she lead a very dull and boring existence. His eyes immediately lit up and he replied that they must do something to make it more interesting. She saw the light of desire in his eyes and it ignited her own passions. She immediately accepted his invitation for a date and they agreed to meet up on the weekend at the local discotheque.

They went out a couple of times and enjoyed their time together. He was warm and friendly and she felt wanted and relaxed in his company. She lived with her widowed mother and often when her mother was out, she would invite him to her house and they spend some wonderful evenings in each other's arms. They talked about their hopes, passions, families, and of course their dreams! He wanted to play cricket for an English county, but had neither the money nor the sponsorship to do that. She, on the other hand, wanted to be a writer, but had no clue how to go about it. They were both young, passionate and talented people who knew just how many obstacles lay on the path to actualizing their goals.

One morning, she dressed herself up and was quite sure this young and handsome cricketer would propose to her, taking their relationship to the next level. She wore her favourite green silk blouse and black skirt which contoured her slim figure. She complimented them with matching emerald drop earrings and a pearl necklace around her slender neck. She looked the picture of perfection guaranteed to melt any man's heart! The doorbell rang at 11.30 am. He walked in, in a sour dull mood. He took her in his arms and made love to her passionately and violently. She had never seen him like this. There was something different about him that day. He was almost like a stranger she never knew! Before she could ask him what was wrong, he brutally told her that he was not over his last relationship and was taking a transfer to another city as he needed some time to himself. She was completely taken aback and stunned by the news. Here she had been dreaming of a future together and he was cruelly tearing her heart to pieces. She never saw him again after that day, and often as she walked down the promenade in the evenings, she would wistfully remember the cricketer who lit up her life, though briefly.

Social Networking

Guess what folks! Social networking sites are hot and happening! For all the lonely people out there, it's your one stop destination to stay connected with your friends, catch up with old ones, and make some new. The first thing I do every morning is not my ablutions, but check up who's dotted the page with their latest updates, events, happenings, and jokes over a cuppa hot steaming tea and Marie biscuits! Believe me when I say that I know what the latest buzz around town is, who's dating whom, who's jetsetting across the globe, what the latest trends in fashion, books, music and movies is, and also what are the best holiday destinations. Besides getting all this, [as if u could ask for more] you also get all the updates on friends, their spouses, their children, and also their pets!

Facebook and Twitter offer instant connectivity to the rest of the world and the virtual world gets more interesting than the real world! My friends list on Facebook currently is at a 111 and rapidly increasing. It's also a sign of one's popularity, if it's real friends you have, not just unknown people. I have a modest figure of 12 followers on twitter, and I am not complaining. Twitter has just come out with a book which is a compilation of the best and funniest and most ingenious tweets, [hope you know what that is!]. There are a lot of celebrity twitters who claim to outdo each other by the number of followers they have. Shashi Tharoor is the one net savvy, uber cool politician who claims to tweet! Now that's a first of its kind. A lot of Bollywood celebrities also claim to tweet, citing their number of followers as an indication of their popularity. However, there are a number of fake profiles too as in the case of Dhoni, the famous cricketer!

These sites never fail to bring a smile on the face as they are also full of funny humorous anecdotes and witty repartees! As a writer, I claim that it's become my one stop source for ideas and one-liners. The play of words coming from a motley group of friends and people who inhabit different spheres of existence and whose reality is very different from the other offers an eclectic mix and play of words, events, and ideas! As a writer, I claim that besides being my dose of stress buster and laughter therapy, it's also a place where novelty and ingenuity co-exist making it a writers treasure hove! I don't know how many of you have profiles on the Net on these networking sites, but if you don't, get one immediately; I can safely vouch for its advantages and assets! The simplest of them—the joy of being connected with your loved ones!

Death of relationship

When a relationship breaks, or when a couple calls it quits, it can really be the singular most traumatising moment in anyone's life. To watch a relationship shatter that you had built together lovingly, is indeed painful. I know that divorces have become common in today's day and age, but to take that final step which will ultimately and untimely sever all ties can be a big challenge in a normal person's life. When we live and share every breathing moment with someone, the other person becomes so much entwined into our lives that to unravel the threads of the relationship itself can take a lifetime. It is impossible to sever a bond in a moment's decision. In a way, the other half, or the better half as we like to call it, becomes a shadow of our own person.

They say that couples start thinking and resembling one another after a period of living together. And it is definitely true. No matter how different we may be, we ultimately start aping each other's likes and dislikes and become like Siamese twins. We are thinking the same thoughts, living the same dreams, and walking on the same life path. A divorce is never easy' hence, because we feel that we are severing a part of our own body and our own existence, there is a hollow and a vacuum, a void that can never be filled again. A divorce would have to be one of the most traumatising events in any individual's life, perhaps more than a person's death. While death is instant and fatal, the scars of a divorce can take years to erase.

Thursday, November 20, 2008

Cesspools of sin!

Metro cities have indeed become cesspools of sleaze, sex, and sin! Coming from a small town myself, I have on numerous occasions had the opportunity to either work in a big city or live there for some time. The observations I have made have indeed shocked me. In the last few years, one has noticed a new kind of permissiveness in these cities, whether it is sex, booze, or drugs. It has percolated down tyo smaller cities also but to a smaller extent!The underbelly of these cities is quite shocking and one is witness to all kind of spurious activities, and sometimes, they are done quite openly in the larger cities and no one bats an eyelid. Drugs and sex are easily available in these cities and people are found to live a very decadent, indulgent, and hedonistic lifestyle. Social boundaries in these cities are quite fluid and the rich and the not so very rich, mingle and party together. The wealth on display in these larger cities is quite shocking as was seen in the case of the Vikram Chatwal–Priya Sachdeva wedding. Festivities continued in Delhi and Jaipur for a fair number of days and the ostentation's and high life was on full display.

The latest movie 'Fashion' by Madhur Bhandarkar also exposes the underbelly of the fashion world, and methinks he has done a brilliant job of it. He has portrayed the exact picture of the reality and one has heard cases of several models who have succumbed to the lure of the glamour world and have lost themselves in the muck of sex, booze, and drugs. The last one heard of them was that they were in rehabilitation.

A new kind of sexual liberation has taken place in India in the last decade. Women are openly flaunting their sexuality, becoming economically independent, and the men are taking full advantage of it. Live-in relationships, pre-marital sex, and even extra-marital affairs are becoming the order of the day. With divorce cases rising in the metros, the institution of marriage seems to be under threat. With working parents, a one child norm in nuclear families seems to be replacing the older joint family system, wherein one had the support of elders in bringing up children. Individualistic attitudes and self seeking tendencies have lead to poorer adjustment with people often going their own ways. With materialism and western lifestyles on the rise, it will be some time before the social order, which is in a constant state of flux, comes to any kind of order and balance. Indians have new social mores and values, and India is definitely changing its social identity very drastically.

Monday, November 17, 2008

Nostalgia

Revisiting one's alma mater always brings back fond memories. The days of girlhood or boyhood are fondly remembered along with the fun one had. The memories are vivid even after years and you feel that those glorious days were just yesterday! I mostly studied in convents, and the quaint charming ways of a convent make it a place safe and cocooned from the real world, where the dreams of girlhood are lived. One remembers the nasty and strict nuns who forbade you to eat the 'forbidden fruits', [no pun intended] outside the imposing iron gates of the school, but which you still managed to sneak out to savour. We remember the naughty friends we shared our lunchboxes with, played games with, and sneaked out to watch movies with. We remember the glorious sports days, when all our sportsman skills were on display, the march pasts, and the cups we won at the end of it all. We remember the concerts where we displayed our prowess of acting and our oratorical skills, the costumes and the stage only preparing us for the larger stage ahead. We remember the fete with the hoopla stalls, the request stall, wherein our sweethearts dedicated songs to us, the boys from the neighbouring schools who exchanged suggestive and naughty glances with us. We remember the foods, the ice *golas,* the scrumptious *chaat,* and of course the burgers and the *tikkis*! It was an era of innocence, of wonder, of hope, of a future filled with new and wondrous experiences, and a life that awaited us young nubile things! Life was rich and fun-filled with laughter, enjoyment, and learning and the love of friends and teachers who guided us gently and sometimes sternly and nudged us toward the right path. It was a time of great creativity, learning and discovering who we were. Those golden days will always be embedded in our memories as days of hope, dreams unlived, and an exciting future that beckoned us.

Thursday, November 13, 2008

Love is a many splendoured thing!

Love is a many splendoured and a magical thing! For anyone who has been hit by the emotion, and most of us have at some point of time been, its a roller coaster ride, when the world appears multi-hued. The world acquires magical proportions and we see everything through rose-tinted glasses. We are on a high, in love not with the object of our desire, but with everything that crosses our paths. There is a rainbow in the sky and rose petals are falling on us from above! Even the most insignificant thing seems loveable and we want to embrace the world as our own.

The chemistry between a man and a woman is an enigmatic and unexplainable thing. When two individuals meet what transpires between them, the sweet nothings whispered and the naughty suggestive glances exchanges create a communication pattern of their own. Lovers have their own unspoken communication. They are oblivious to the world and for a period of time, they are the key players of this cosmos and only and only they matter. Every other matter and issue takes a back seat.

But love is not always a cakewalk. We do suffer agonies of separation, betrayal, loss and hurt in love. Even the slightest snub or reprimand by our loved one can cause us heartache like none other. Oh, do we yearn for our loved on when we are apart. Don't we wish for his or her sweet presence and soft caress. And if our loved one were to betray us or fall out of love with us, woe betide us. Lovers can also be merciless and cause us to suffer endlessly. When one is in love, we become a puppet in the hands of our lover. Our lover can manipulate us and humiliate us and we bear in silence.

Such are the shades of love. A lot has been written about love and poets and writers have devoted pages to unravel its mystery. Yet, it remains an enigma. Love, they say is blind and it often eludes us. But for those happy and fortunate ones who do find everlasting world, the world is a better place because of it.

Sunday, November 9, 2008

A Land of contrasts

The rift between the rich and poor continues to widen. Why are the rich getting richer and the poor poorer? The rich flaunt lifestyles that are hedonistic, lavishly obscene, and materialistic. In contrast, the poor are on the streets with no housing, no basic rights, begging for a few morsels of food to fill up their empty, bloating stomachs. The contrasts are hugely visible in large cities, which are meccas of gold on one hand and gutters of slime, filth, squalor, and poverty on the other.

A land of contrasts, we have always been. In ancient India, lives of royalty with unimaginable wealth and grandeur ruled the land, while the common man remained shrouded in poverty. Legends of India being the land of riches, untold wealth, snake charmers, elephants, the sacred cow, and of course the poor fakir, did the rounds. Fallacies about our country abounded and it is only now, in the past ten years, that certain myths about our country have begun to crumble. India has suddenly come into its own as a land of technological advances, where the ancient coexists with the modern. India is a land of extremes and of contradictions. Ancient beliefs conflict with more modern values. Joint families are facing the threat of nuclear families and traditions are under attack!

India has undergone tremendous transformation. Its rise to a country of power and prominence has been meteoric and the stuff legends are made of. The benefits of the new age economy are there for all to see. Urban India is reaping the benefits, fast and furious. Smaller towns and villages are still waking up to these colossal changes. Villages continue to reel under farmer suicides, malnutrition, and hunger. Can we, in this scenario, claim to be a world power? Can we claim that our time under the sun is here? Yes, definitely, this is because India is a land of contrasts and will always be.

Saturday, November 8, 2008

I have a dream!

I dream a lot. No, I am not talking about dreams you have in your real life, like seeing your children grow into productive adults, or then about owning a dream house, or then rising to become the CEO of your company. Sure, I have these dreams too, but right now, I am talking about the dreams you have during the night's sleep. The kind you have not in your waking moments, but when you have lost consciousness of the real world and the inner world takes over.

My dreams are very vivid; in fact, they would almost seem real. Last night, I dreamt that my sister was performing at a circus with little kids and her pants caught fire. Now, why in the world would I like to see her suffer such indignities! The night before, I dreamt that we had been taken over by a gang of terrorists, who were actually aliens, and they planted chips on us humans, which tracked our movement and made us slaves to their commands. Now what could possibly be the logical explanation for dreams such as these?!

I read Freud's 'Interpretation of Dreams' and it made no sense to me. I don't want to go into the politics of sexual libido behind the dreams, as he puts it. I sit every morning and jot down my dreams, as psychologists suggest we do, as we tend to forget them very fast.

Some dreams are, however, very realistic, and I often meet old forgotten friends and relatives in my dreams and revisit old memories and places. Often, I find the solution to a long impending problem in my dream and a problem resolves itself. The mechanism of the mind is a complex and mesmerising issue. The abilities and the potential of the human mind is limitless. So, I say, keep dreaming and wake up each morning to a fresh new world.

The world order

The world order is constantly in a state of flux. What may be the reality today may not be so tomorrow. This just goes to show the speed the world is changing at and the rate at which events are taking place. One has to run to stand in the same place. No more can we rest on our laurels as events and happenings overtake us at breakneck speed.

Are there any absolutes in this world? I believe, no. Everything can be questioned and deconstructed. There is an equal and opposing viewpoint to every story. Someone who is a success today may not remain so tomorrow. Welcome to the world of cut-throat competitiveness.

When I started blogging, someone asked me what will you blog about? Have you thought of a subject?

From the looks of it, everyone is blogging these days and writing about every thing under the sun. So, what makes a blog successful? Is it the language, the theme, the vocabulary, that makes it interesting? I believe it is the writer's voice that comes through clearly in a piece of writing that makes a blog or writing successful. The writing should have the distinctive stamp of the author. And of course, consistency makes a writer successful. Not just erratic, spontaneous, sporadic, momentary outpourings of creativity, which of course I am highly guilty of.

Monday, June 1, 2009

The rejection slip

'You fancy yourself to be a writer?' he said. The derision and condescension in his voice stung me like cold water thrown over the face. The barb hurt badly! I write because I must, I thought self-defensively. I always found myself defending my speech, my thoughts, and actions to everyone ever since I can remember. Unfortunately, an artist feels more than he thinks. Only the consciousness is important. I had always followed the stream of consciousness kind of writing. Did it connect with reality? Maybe not, but then writers live in a mental prison of their own making!

What makes an artist? An abstraction of the concrete or a concretisation of the abstract? How does one justify the fact that some talent never sees the light of day? Does that in any way take away from the brilliance of the artist? Does he cease to exist? Who decides whether a work of art is good or bad? Do market forces rule the world of art too? Should we give in to commercial interests? Should we give in to the casting couch? Should an artist sell his soul? Does he really need a stamp of approval? But then who gives him that seal of approval-society, mammon, or then the Devil himself?

Is genius doomed to anonymity and self destruction? So what good is genius? Isn't it more a curse than a gift? Mediocrity survives while genius dies! So why not be mediocre and live in a safe haven? Eat, drink, and be merry like everyone else. Why suffer? Why feel that you have a point to prove? Who cares anyway?

I wrote for a fortnightly till the editor told me I couldn't write. I worked for the English supplement of a Hindi newspaper that nobody ever read! Of late, I have become increasingly self conscious of my art. Did Salman Rushdie think of the Fatwa when he wrote his blasphemous work? John Keats died an early death because critics panned his work! Today, he is hailed as a great! Is life really fair?

'So you think u can write? Think again lady!' said he, as he flung the neatly typed manuscript across the table. Another rejection, another disappointment, thought I, as I walked out of the plush office. Am I a failed artist?

....

Wednesday, May 20, 2009

Difficult situations and how we overcome them

A person's life is never a bed of roses and during one's lifetime, one does encounter a lot of ups and downs and one has to gear up to face the problems head on. As they say, when u throw someone into the water they learn to swim; so too it is in the case of problems. One may find the problem too overwhelming, but one gradually acquires the skills to overcome them. Similarly, I too have faced several difficulties in my life and I will gradually outline them.

To begin with, my childhood was fun-filled and easy going, but as I reached adulthood, I began to face problems I had no skills to manage. When I joined college in Mumbai, I was a small town girl, out in the world on my own for the first time. I found commuting in the huge mega polis very difficult and it was something I definitely had to get used to, and it came through practice and overcoming my fear of the crowds. Then, in college, I sought a counsellor to help guide me through the process of selecting the right subjects for my major. I had to find a place for myself in the hostel and learn to adjust with the other girls and the rules and regulations. It took me some time but then I gradually adjusted. The experience was difficult, but it was an eye-opener to a new kind of life.

Later on in life, after I had been through several jobs and a marriage, I found myself heading for a divorce. It was a difficult, traumatic period, but I sought the company of friends and self help books to tide over the crisis. Even today, although I live alone and have a negligible social life, I tend to network over the net and have a large number of friends on Facebook, with whom I share my life. One has to establish a large network of friends and a solid support system. I am also a part of a writers group, in which my passion for writing and sharing with like minded people comes to the fore.

Also, I take a long time to recharge my batteries if I happen to be suffering from stress. I sleep a lot, eat right, exercise, listen to music, and retreat to a space of my own within myself. I do a lot of soul

119

searching and eventually come up with a solution to the problem. I also try and see the situation from a different angle and try to see the blessing in disguise in it. I also sleep a lot, and this relaxes me completely.

Also, when I sleep I dream a lot. I see bizarre, complex dreams and these generally hold the solution to a problem I may be suffering from. I have a book with the help of which I analyze my dreams. This procedure helps me a lot and is very therapeutic and healing. My dreams are very vivid and I note them down the first thing in the morning as we tend to forget our dreams very fast. My dreams have helped me resolve difficult issues and any major issue or wish fulfilment gets sorted out in my dreams.

So these are some ways in which our problems get resolved. I also meditate and practice yoga. This helps me to calm down considerably and removes stress. One should also believe in the higher power and understand that God is always there to watch over us and this is probably his way of testing us. So, believe in spirituality, in a life beyond, eat healthy, think healthy, and don't let negative thoughts overrun you and you will go a long way.

Baap of all blogs!

I have been surfing the net several nights at a stretch and have come across blogs of such worth and presence that my blog pales in comparison. I am frankly amazed at the talent that abounds and am taken aback at the creativity and expertise of folks on subjects varied. As far as Indian blogs are concerned, I am stupefied by the knowledge of the ordinary bloke [if we may call him that], his expert comments, and analysis on all things topical, be it the general elections of 2009, or Indian cinema, or then the state of economic affairs. From a literary standpoint, some of the blogs I have personally loved have been Sonia Faleiro's blog and Amitav Kumar's blog, both writers of repute and standing. Then there are the random blogs with comments on everything under the sun, and one is dumbfounded by the standard of language used and the levels of creativity. I have always been taken back by the skill of the average educated Indian with the Queen's English though it would be unfair to call it that anymore. The English language is now so deeply entrenched in the Indian psyche as the first language for many educated Indians. Indians have evolved their own brand of the language, with its own grammar, its own intonations, its own accent, own local lingo, which has contributed greatly to the enhancement of the English language. A language reflects a nation's culture and sensibilities, and it would be fair to say that Indian English, which is not too diverse from the standard English, has come into its own.

It is interesting to see a language evolve just as it is interesting to see a young nation carve an identity of its own and emerge as a strong force to reckon with in the world scene. India has made great progress, be it in the economic field, in arts, culture, etc., and is known the world over for its economics, its intellectuals, its artists, its films, its democracy, its diversity, and above all, for its talent pool of skilled trained professional who are motivated to succeed and are hardworking. Popular perceptions of India as a poverty ridden, backward country, of snake charmers, elephants, old defunct rituals and traditions, and the now extinct tiger are now being challenged and exploded. India has come into its own and the old world order of western dominance is slowly and surely crumbling. India is a good place to be in now, and its 100 billion odd population, which is spread all over the world, is making its mark quietly.

There is then, our 'Hinglish', which is a very *desi* version of the language, with smatterings of Hindi thrown in. A lot of idioms are borrowed heavily from popular culture, inspired by Bollywood, and sometimes college, local, and regional lingo. Shobhaa De, a popular columnist, makes use of this *Hinglish* heavily in her columns, which appear in a leading English daily. Bollywood is of course an offshoot of Hollywood, to assume that Hollywood is a *baap* of all filmdom. The term Bollywood, often considered deriding by many a cine stars, Amitabh Bachchan included, has finally gained acceptability and credence by being included in the Oxford dictionary of late.

....

Thursday, April 2, 2009

The Happiness quotient

I was watching a programme on the quest for happiness by Deepak Chopra, the world renowned spiritual guru, today. It was an insightful programme on how to attain happiness in our lives. A lot of us are constantly seeking the eternal question as to how to attain a higher lever of consciousness and happiness and spiritual peace and bliss. Surprisingly, our living conditions contribute to only 8% of our happiness quotient. We can be as happy as we choose to be irrespective of our living conditions. Our mind has a set point which determines how happy we are. Also, the voluntary actions we choose to take in our lives determine how happy we are to be.

For many people happiness is an elusive dream. They are constantly asking the perennial existential question—what is the reason for our existence? But, surprisingly, happiness has nothing to do with material possessions. A true glass of champagne, sex, or a reckless bout of shopping can give us happiness, but this is only momentary. Happiness is eventually a state of mind and we can choose to be happy under any given conditions. There are hormones in the brain which are called happiness hormones which get released and give us the kind of high we would experience were we in love, had sex, or eaten chocolates!

So, eventually, we all have to find our own answers and seek our own happiness. We have to focus on our health, attain a higher level of consciousness, and choose to be happy. We are all eventually responsible for our own happiness. So go out there, live each day, and smile, make others happy, and spread cheer in this world and you will find happiness. It's finally a bluebird sitting in your own backyard! Catch it before it flies away.

Friday, March 13, 2009

Dilli-6

This would definitely have to be one of the most fascinating and brilliant films I have seen in a long time. All kudos to Rakeysh Mehra of 'Aks' and 'Rang De Basanti' fame for making a film that strikes a chord in the heart of every Indian. The film is completely Indian in soul and portrays the character of the city of Delhi with all its complexities, layers, and cultural richness.

The movie revolves around the character of an old woman, played by Waheeda Rehman, who wants to breathe her last in her own land and travels from the West back to India, accompanied by her grandson, played by Abhishek Bachchan. She longs for her roots and rediscovers them in her old ancestral home in the narrow gullies of old Delhi and among her long lost relatives. Abhishek is an outsider all this time and finds Delhi, beguiling, if not a little confusing and perplexing.

All the characters in the film have been etched brilliantly, be it the low-caste sweeper, '*Jalebi*', played by Divya Dutta, who is shunned and ostracised by everyone, the corrupt police constable, the Muslim shopkeeper, Abhishek's parent's old friend, Rishi Kapoor, who gives pearls of wisdom to the younger man, Abhishek, on love and life gained from his own experiences. The love interest is played by Sonam Kapoor, who plays an aspirant for the Indian idol competition. The sleazy politician played by Prem Chopra, who has a younger wife who is always decked in gold to portray his status, and finally, the sleazy photographer who sleeps with other men's wives.

A lot of stories are played out parallel to the main story of Abhishek being lost in the labyrinth of subterfuge, psychological drama, corruption, and religious and political themes. The symbol of the '*Kala Bandar*', a real life incident of Delhi, is a parable to showcase the black monkey that lives within all of us and rears its ugly head every now and then. People are involved in heavy discussion as to how to overpower this monkey menace, with little thought to the monkey that lives within. The climax of the film is complicated with a near riot in the by lanes of Old Delhi, where the Hindus and Muslims coexist, sometimes not so harmoniously. Abhishek intervenes in his own ingenious way to save the neighbourhood from the flames of religious hatred and in the process also rescues his lady love Sonam, who is out to escape a forced arranged marriage by running away to Mumbai with the sleazy photographer. Abhishek gets shot at in the melee that follows and everyone watches with bated breath while the story takes a happy ending.

So, finally, it takes a foreigner in the form of Abhishek to stress the values of love and brotherhood and forces us to look within and question our values, customs, and traditions. It would be foolish not to mention the Ramleela, that is so much a part of the Hindu culture and which is played out in the storyline to depict he rich cultural life of Delhi. A remarkable film with a mind blowing sound track, that is sure to hit every Indian at his core. A movie very Indian in its soul which is sure to be loved by many as an artistic endeavour that rises to cinematic excellence.

Friday, February 6, 2009

Slumdog milionaire

I finally watched the movie today. Couldn't understand what the brouhaha was about. It's a very average film with some interesting scenes portraying the underbelly of Mumbai life. On the whole, it is a story about an underdog, who gets lucky every time he is in a mess and emerges the winner of a crore of rupees on a game show. The acting by first time actor Dev Patel who plays the protagonist Jamal and Frieda Pinto as Latika and not to forget Anil Kapoor as the game show host, is excellent and each has portrayed their role very naturally and realistically. I don't quite agree with the notion that this movie sells poverty to the West. True, the scenes of poverty and grime will seem very exotic to the Western eye, but at the end of the day, it's simply a movie and a work of art.

The childhood scenes of Jamal and his brother Salim rise to a level of cinematic excellence and that's all I can say about the film. But the film could have been set anywhere, in Mexico, Brazil, or any other South American city. The scenes were reminiscent of such places and the incidents portrayed were out of a novella and could have been out of a Charles Dickens book on the exploitation of children. There was nothing that was unique to India.

Indians on the whole will not identify with the film, especially the poverty and the slum life that is shown. Indians on the whole have become a little too prosperous and the average middle class Indian is as removed from poverty as his Western counterpart. But nowhere in the film does one feel that India is being portrayed in a negative light. The reactions that have been coming have been by far too extreme and jingoistic. At the end of the day, it's a film, which may or may not be true to reality and is a work of art. Should be taken as that!

Saturday, January 10, 2009

Mid- life blues

As one approaches the mid-thirties one is hit by what is commonly termed as mid-life blues. One has made some decisions by this time regarding marriage, career, and other such important matters. One looks back and tries to assess where one is now. One can become disappointed and dissatisfied with life at this stage. One either wants more out of life, or one is just not satisfied with their current situations and relationships. Weight begins to creep up and some little grey hair begin to appear. One is truly and completely past their youth which was such a golden period in their life. Relinquishing one's youth and the realisation that youth is now past is definitely one of the most difficult matters to confront. Young people begin calling one the dreaded word, 'Aunty' which one completely shuns and abhors. It's a sad realisation that one is now well past one's prime and has to make way for the younger lot.

Romance has gone out of life and marriage and is replaced by larger concerns of career, children's finances, and other such important and pressing matters. Responsibilities have increased and we realise that time is no longer ours. We are either running around kids and family or performing familial duties. The carefree days of youth are surely and definitely over. Acceptance of the current situation is one way to tide over mid-life blues. One has to learn to accept that one is no longer carefree and unburdened by life's responsibilities but has people who now depend on them.

As we enter a new phase of life, one has to gradually phase oneself to deal with what life churns out and learn to be positive and happy.

Wednesday, January 7, 2009

Old is gold!

I have recently been meeting a lot of old friends from school after ages, and it's very fascinating to know how most of them have evolved! It's fun to watch girls who were non-entities in school and were the invisible back-benchers, who are now smart confident, accomplished women. It's interesting to watch the ugly ducklings who have made successful marriages and are leading happy fulfilled marriages. It's most beguiling to watch the class topper who is languishing in the dark somewhere. It's interesting to watch the class brains who are struggling with jobs and some others who are leading the single life struggling with life and their careers. It's fascinating to watch the life path each one has taken and how they have eventually evolved. Each person comes as an eye-opener and teaches you a lesson. Most of the girls I met have moved on to different parts of the world while some are still languishing in their hometown. This some would include me. Most of my friends who knew me back in school as the restless, adventurous one are surprised to see me still in my hometown. Well, its not that I haven't moved out in all these years, but its just that I eventually landed back here! Maybe I just love this ol' town of mine, or then maybe I am just a small town girl at heart.

We all leave school with big dreams in our eyes and how many of us do finally realise our dreams. Some of us just want to get married and raise kids, while some of us are more ambitious and adventurous. How many of us succeed and how many of us fall by the wayside is another reality. Life takes its own course for most of us and while some move on to higher planes, some of us fall by the wayside. Some of us are lucky at the first shot, while others struggle for a longer time to make the cut. It's fun to catch up with old friends at reunions, and many feel that reunions are only for the successful and the others should stay at home. A very cruel thought indeed. However, it's a blessing to meet your old friends and reconnect with them and share your stories with them.

Wednesday, December 31, 2008

The New Year!

As we herald in the New Year, there is a new kind of optimism in the air and it's time to leave out the old and ring in the new. As the year draws to a close we are clinging on to old habits and older memories. Many relationships have jaded out and many lost their meaning. The New Year is the time to form new bonds, make new resolutions, break out of old habits and thought patterns and embrace new ones. We have to break out of old systems and usher in the change that we most need. The New Year is the time we asses our lives, the directions we are taking, and the new journeys we are beginning. We are on a new road that is not littered with obstacles, but which is full of new hope, opportunities, and optimism! We have the chance once again to reassess our lives, leave out by the wayside all that is unwanted and obsolete, and make promises of new beginnings. We have to smell the roses along the way and take in the beautiful scent of the flowers that line our path. It's a time for new agendas, a new focus in life, and time to recharge our lives and take stock of where we are headed and if the values we have chosen to guide us are right and to reasses our choices.

May this year, 2009, be absolutely stunning and wonderful for everyone, and may each and all fulfil their dreams this year. May this year be special for all and all fears, worries and stress be just a thing of the past like the last year! May we all be safe in our homes, in our jobs, and in this land that we live. May no strangers and enemies come and destroy our peace and happiness.

Friday, November 7, 2008

A free land!

I just got back this morning from a beautiful trip to, Auroville, which is about a 20-minutes drive away from Pondicherry. Pondicherry was a French colony and the remnants of the French culture are still there to see. It's an idyllic sea side town, with postcard picturesqueness. Auroville is an international town, which is being promoted as an ideal town where there is no religion, no caste, no creed and above all no hierarchy. It is a town where money is not the lord. People come from all over the world to soak up the sun and laze on the beaches, but above all to expand their consciousness and to be in harmony with nature. They meditate, they serve humanity, and they live a simple existence in peace and harmony. Hence, it is an international community, dedicated to the service of humanity. It is a picturesque town with international class boutiques, where hand made products such as incense sticks, bath soaps, perfumes, stationary, and also clothes and accessories are stocked. The Aurobindo Ashram is located in Pondicherry and houses photographs of the seer and his *samadhi* and books about his teachings and philosophy as well.

Auroville is also the location of the Matrimandir, which is in the shape of a golden globe, where people congregate to meditate and reach a higher level of consciousness. Auroville was an eye-opener to an international way of existence and of living in harmony with nature. Almost 2 million trees have been planted to give the place a green cover which keeps it in harmony with the ecosystem. Above all it is a beautiful place, a getaway from the noisy stressful, polluted city life we are used to.

Tuesday, December 16, 2008

The Mother of all Vamps!

Yeah, I am talking about the mother of all vamps! The one and only Silk Smitha, if you have heard of her, which I am quite sure you have. In case you are an ignoramus, let me update you that she 'was' [yes, unfortunately she is no more] one of the sexiest sirens down south and in fact in the whole of India. She has been given the title Silk Smitha by the South Indian industry and her fans, of course. She was quite deadly, if you have watched her in action in one of those seedy South Indian movies wherein the women are voluptuous if not humongous and they have flesh in all the right places! Yes, seedy they surely look, but they offer enough entertainment to those front benchers who get their *'paisavasool'*, in the form of an erection, if nothing else! [Sorry for being gross!]

I was just thinking about this particular woman and how she eventually died an ignominious death, as she committed suicide. The path to stardom and fame for many such women is littered with heartbreaks and humiliation. Often abandoned by their poor families and left to fend for themselves at a tender age, these women fall victim to the evil eye of men who exploit them for their own lecherous means. Well I will not enter the territory of men bashing here, that we will leave for another post. The casting couch which does exist in the film world sounds the death-knell of such women. In their race for money and fame, they fall prey to such incidents and often end up losing their peace of mind. The struggle is harsh and the world of men is even harsher. Silk Smitha, who lit up the South Indian screen for a short time, has indeed left her mark as a seductress and a siren, and I am sure that many of her fans remember her with a tear in their eyes.

Saturday, December 13, 2008

Thecha!

Gotcha! You must be wondering what on earth am I talking about. After all her serious posts, has this blog writer gone stark, raving mad? Na! I am just raving about an exotic food preparation today. The one Maharashtrains call *Thecha*! It accompanies every typical Maharashtrain fare. What is it made of? Well, this exotic chutney, if I may call it that, is made of the most hot, sizzling fresh red chillies, bought freshly off the supermarket. The sight of those attractive red chillies is enough to make your mouth and eyes water and conjure up the most exciting and hot dishes one can possibly think of.

I bought some today and promptly instructed my maid to make the exotic preparation. She washed the fresh shining bright red chillies and added oil, some garlic, and salt to it and blended it in a mixer. The most delicious aroma wafted through as she opened the cover of the blender. She made some *jowar rotis* as accompaniments and I enjoyed a mouth watering meal of the simple yet tantalising *Thecha* with *jowar rotis*. It is indeed a poor man's food, but enough to make any rich man put aside all other dishes to try a taste of this exciting chutney. I hope you make some tonight and try it too! Adios!

Saturday, December 6, 2008

Shallow Hal!

I watched a movie last night. It was probably called Shallow Hal. It starred Gwyneth Paltrow and explores the touchy subject of people's obsession with outer appearances. The lead character, a young guy, is obsessed with outer physical appearances and this makes him a rather shallow man. He is having difficulties with his relationships and a mind expert he meets accidentally in a lift, hypnotises him into believing that women are better looking than what they are in reality. His perception gets altered and he sees average even downright ugly women as beautiful. In the meantime he meets Gwyneth Paltrow, who is a ridiculously obese woman and sees her as this sexy gorgeous woman. He dates her and eventually falls in love with her. Her father is the director of the firm he works for and during a casual meeting over dinner Hal impresses him with some unique and clever ideas and her father promptly promotes him in the company. Everybody believes that Hal is dating the boss's ugly and fat daughter only for his job.

In the meantime, Hal's friend, who is quite upset with his friend dating losers, meets up with the mind expert and convinces him to redo the hypnosis he had performed on Hal's mind. Hal regains his original perception and all chaos breaks loose. He walks out on Gwyneth in a restaurant after failing to recognise her. He refuses to take her calls and even meet her fearing what he may see. After seeing him with a pretty young thing in a restaurant, Gwyneth's character, whose heart is broken, chooses to go join the peace corps. Hal eventually realises that he truly and really loves Gwyneth irrespective of her appearance and finally makes it up to her.

The movie is a touching one that makes you think. In this day and age where society is obsessed with outer beauty and perfection, it came across as a sweet, charming film. We have a culture where anorexic women are obsessed with size zero and outer beauty is all that matters. This film gave the message that we should not judge a book by its cover and that inner beauty is more important than what lies on the outside. Definitely something to think about!

Sunday, November 30, 2008

Ah Taj!

The sight of the Taj building burning and being under siege seared my heart. The beautiful heritage building was being bombarded with grenade launchers and fires were burning down every part of the building. My heart went out to every person who was trapped inside that massive structure. As images of the burning building played on the television screen and I watched with horror, numb and helpless at the mindlessness of it all, my heart went out to the friends and family of those killed and the many trapped inside the Taj.

Terrorists who were described as kids, by the eyewitnesses entered the Taj from the Gateway of India and took the building under their control. They opened indiscriminate fire at the staffers and guests in the lobby and the Shamiana, which is a 24-hour coffee shop and where patrons walk in casually at all times of the day to have a cup of coffee. The Taj is one of the most oft-visited and popular haunts for visitors to Mumbai and anyone visiting Mumbai has to make a trip to the grand monument, even if its just to have a coffee or a sandwich and stroll through its luxurious halls, restaurants, and lobby. Visitors insisted on being given the 'sunview' suite which overlooked the sea. That is exactly where the TOI journalist Sabina Sakia was staying when her room was razed to the ground when a terrorist threw a grenade in that wing of the hotel.

There are many survivor stories to recount of children being separated from their parents, of couples losing their spouse, as in the case of the GM of the Taj, who was attending the call of duty while his wife and two children burned to death at the 6th floor of the hotel. Guests tried to escape from the hotel using curtains as makeshift ropes to climb out of their rooms. Guests were escorted out of the restaurants which were under attack by the staff members from service passages and secret exits. The horror tales are many, and survivors recount their narrow escape from the clutches of sure death days after the actual attack.

It was heartbreaking indeed to see the beautiful structure of the hotel which has been an iconic monument and a very prominent landmark of Mumbai, which is a symbol of luxury, beauty, and pride for all Mumbaikars being devastated in this manner! The terrorists knew their game plan well and were very aware of the layout of the hotel. The NSG commandos who entered the hotel to counter the terrorists were lost in the maze of rooms and corridors and had difficulty in accessing the labyrinth of passages that the Taj is comprised of. Many talked about the involvement of hotel staff in the attacks, but the management has categorically denied any such thing.

My heart broke as I watched the pictures of the burning and devastated Taj on the television screen and it was indeed a throwback to the 9/11 attacks of New York when the twin towers were razed to the ground. The scenes were horrific and a reminder of that tragedy. Luckily the loss of lives was not so large and the terrorists who planned to take as many lives as possible were timely intercepted and brought to their death. It was indeed a traumatic event for all Indians to see their country under attack and to see so many innocent lives being tragically and senselessly lost.

Thursday, November 27, 2008

Terror Attacks!

Terror has permeated every corner of the world and we Indians are no longer immune to it. It is definitely a new phenomenon and Indians are slowly but surely waking up to the new phenomena and gearing up to deal with the new reality. The terror attacks on Mumbai, the commercial capital of the country, on the 26th Nov 2008 were indeed dastardly and heinous. The attacks carried out on some of the most prominent places of Mumbai were targeted to kill innocent civilians and destroy public property and create fear and panic among the residents of the city. The terror attacks were unforeseen and a lot of innocent lives were lost in the bargain, especially at the Taj hotel, the Trident hotel, Nariman House, Chattrapati Shivaji Terminus, Colaba, and the old Leopold cafe. Young professionals, innocent bystanders, residents, passers-by and not to forget the brave and valiant policemen on duty, were killed in the attack.

The attack made headlines all across the world and the news was splashed prominently on newspaper cover pages as foreign citizens and nationals were also involved. Especially in the hotels, reports leaked out that American and British nationals were being targeted. Elsewhere at Nariman House, Israeli nationals were taken hostages. The terrorists were Muslims and presumably from Pakistan and were armed with the latest weaponry and ammunitions. They entered Mumbai from the Arabian Sea on a raft and their entry point was the Gateway of India.

This latest terror attack, in which almost 130 people have been reported killed and almost 300 injured, has left the nation shocked. Politicians from across the country cutting across political barriers flew down to Mumbai to take stock of the situation. They also visited the injured who have been hospitalised at the JJ Hospital in Mumbai. The nation needs to wake up to this new threat to the nation, and the government needs to come down strongly on the groups involved. The government has played soft on terror for a long time and now is the time for some tough and stern action.

Mumbai, the city that never sleeps, has gone into deep slumber since these attacks, but it will not be long before it rises like a Phoenix from the ashes and gears itself to face the new threat to its existence. Mumbai has faced a lot of difficult times in the past, such an the riots, the underworld, gang wars, the local train bomb blasts, but each time it has bounced back with resilience and gusto to face life full on.

Sunday, November 23, 2008

The Devil's advocate.

Why is it that we always fall in love with the wrong person? What is it, - a case of attraction of the opposites. True, opposites do attract, and they attract very strongly, but they also create a lot of noise together. The chemistry between two opposites is always great, it's like two worlds who are perpetually on a collision course and in the process there are a lot of sparks, helluva lot of fire, sizzling passion, and an ear-deafening explosion! But does this attraction last? And what is it that one looses in the process? Well, only a little bit of pride, which definitely goes for a toss, and all your values and beliefs are in for an overhaul. All the things that you believed in so staunchly seem a little unrealistic now, and matters which were your priorities earlier take the backseat.

When you emerge from a relationship such as described above not only are you scathed but you emerge a different person than the one you were when you entered the relationship. You have grown, you have learnt, and the world that you so sacredly clung on to, seems a little lop-sided! Your views, values and prejudices take a back-seat and you are left wondering if you made any sense at all, in the first place.

It always takes two people to make sense, just as it takes two to clap and definitely two to tango. So why is living alone so difficult? You have no one to validate what you feel and think, and there is no-one to witness the life that you so dearly call your own. Marriage has its own benefits no matter what the die-hard cynics tell you. It gives you comfort and a sense of security, a sense of acceptance, and validates your existence. Those who plead for the cause of the single man or woman or who say that the single man travels the farthest and the fastest, failed to take into account the loneliness involved. Life is not about arriving at a destination, but it is also about the journey, and a partner makes the journey all the more pleasurable and worth the while. It is rightly said, in sickness and in health, till death do us part, and it is only when we are a little older, that we realise the wisdom in these simple words

Thursday, March 25, 2010

All for Love and much more!

A lots been happening in India of late. The IPL, the womens reservation bill, the indo-pak talk, the controversies Big B inadvertantly gets into and much more. The IPL has created a buzz around the nation and even though its peak summer and exam time, people of all ages are flocking to watch the matches. There are however some oddballs like me who have absolutely zero interest in the game. I cant get quite beyond identifying SRK and his night riders , maybe a Sachin Tendulkar and a noodle strapped Mandira Bedi. The rest can disappear into oblivion for all i care ! The white cheerleaders however caught my attention and i wondered did we really need white babes to up the glamour quotient. Wer'nt our desi equivalent good enough. Or then there was a ned to give this tournament a truly international flavour and hence the sexy girls from across the shores! Drum beats, cheerleaders, sixes and fours, fashion shows all night partying and India is truly a happening place. There is a lot of money involved too and cricketers are becoming huge celebrities overnight, faster than the runs they score!

Somewhere else in parliament, the womens reservation bill was passed. There was a lot of opposition to it, but it eventually saw the light of day. Women hope to benefit from this bill which will see 33% representation of women in parliament. How thee archaic men react to it remains to be seen. It however remains a very positive move in the emancipation of women and their legal representation across boards.

Big B courts controversy everyday. If it isnt for his blog and his frequent run ins with journalists , he is the father of controversies himself. Being a spokesman for Mulayam Singhs UP got him into trouble and if that wasnt enough being Gujrats brand ambassador for Narendra Modi earned him more negative votes with the congress. Even if the man sneezes, it makes news and causes many a thrones to rock and umpteen upheavals. I think like MF Hussain , it will soon be impossible for him to live in this country what with different factions pulling him in different directions.Luckily he commands a huge fan following and like SRk remains extremely welcome and loved in this country.

M F Hussain has absconded to Qatar and evaded arrest and the numerous cases against him for painting Hindu goddesses in an obscene manner. Many intellectuals have come forward in his favour saying he is a man of immense genius and should be let off the hook. However he has enraged the masses and the Hindu factions and will if nothing else have to explain his actions. He however continues to live in luxury in Doha and paints feverishly even at this ripe old age. I say may they make more like him.His creativity truly knows no bounds, love him or then hate him!

Summer catches on in India. Its the season of power cuts, hot weather and water woes in a lot of places.These are some of the key issues India needs to tackle if it needs to call itself a truly developed nation. Coolers, water melons, Khus sherbatss come on the scene and its time for lazy langurous siestas in the afternoons. Its exam time and then the kids are off either to their grandparentss homes or then to foreign destinations for holidays.

Soap operas on the telly continue to be women centric. However there is a sea change in how women are being portrayed post Balaji telefilms and Ekta, the enfant terrible off Indian telly. Womens issues, like widow remarriage, child marriage, feudal systems and its opression, women leaders and then again simple ideal homemakers fighting everyday problems are being sensitively portrayed.Indian telly has never had it better.Gone are the vicious and vacuous Saas Bahu soaps and taking their place are educative and sensitising serials.

Inbdia has truly made its mark globally. Indian food, movies and fashion are now on the global scene.Our art and culture loved all over. Our diaspora is making waves overseas.

Talking of films a new movie,' *Love Sex Dhoka'* is creating a buzz.

It takes a look at relationships in a new light and the new liberal attitude of Indians towards sex and relationships in urban and small town India.A show titled Emotional Attyachar is doing the rounds on the telly and shows how a large percentage of Indians cheat if given the opportunity. This is the new morality in India and its India in the throes of a sexual revolution which is redefining lifestyles.

All this and lots more.Our neighbours are creating trouble once again by not being cooperative in combing out terrorists.Its high time India adopted a tough stand and caught the bull by the horns!

Till i meet u again Adios!

POEMS

Poetry fascinates me!

An idiot in love!
Fumbling and bumbling,
I grope for words,
I call myself a writer?!
Then why this verbal constipation?

I needed to say the right words,
For that much needed effect!
But words fail me,
And I am left flailing like a pathetic weakling!

You stand tall beside me,
And I feel the temperature rising!
Why is it that you have this effect on me?
When all I can do is gawk!

Your presence ignites me,
And I am quivering like jelly!
You watch every move I make,
And I melt like cheese!

You touch my hand,
And I jerk it away.
When all I want,
Is for you to smother my mouth!

I trip over my heels,
And land in your arms!
You save me from falling flat,
When all I want is to fall head over heels!

My first attempts at poetry

Why do I feel this way?
Despair, hopelessness, a sense of emptiness,
Why do I feel this way?
Long lonely days and lonelier nights,
Who do I want by my side?

Fame, glory, achievements,
Why do they seem so transient?
Happy faces around me,
Why does nothing seem to satisfy me?

Eternal seeker, sceptic,
Why cant I take life for what it is?
Is life an endless journey,
With no destination in sight!

I saw the light at the end of the dark tunnel,
I held out my hand,
Save my soul dear God,
Before I get lost in this Neverland!

Waiting

Was this love not meant to be?
Then why did u cast your spell on me?
Bewitching me,
Benumbing me!

Like a lily-livered kitten,
I purred in front of you,
Weak in the knees,
Woozy in the brains!

I walked the night,
Without any lights,
The wind in my hair,
And the rain on my cheeks!

You didn't come to me,
Left me high and dry,
Yearning for you,
Aching in the night!

Spring

The bug buzzing around my head,
The grasshopper on the lawn,
The *koel* on the branch,
The butterfly on the rose!

Come spring, u are welcome,
After the long dreary winter,
Come awaken my desires,
Which have been hibernating for long!

The sprightly deer in the park,
The tiger cub in the pond,
The peacock in its attire,
All welcome ure new dawn!

Come light my fires,
Whose embers are smouldering in the dark,
Come into my life,
And bring the spring back into my step!

Happenings!

Things happening around us,
Reality changing fast,
What was, is no longer so,
And a new presence is in its place!

MJ died and was buried in Neverland,
A new pathway in the middle of Mumbai,
Twitter, Facebook, new connections,
My old safe world is topsy turvy!

I am no longer who I used to be,
There is an awareness of a new me,
New beginnings, death of old habits,
Who is this mellow, mature, me!

Lessons learnt,
Old friends forgotten,
New faces,
There is a strangeness in place of the old familiarity!

Will I survive the change,
Places I have been to,
Live in my memory forever,
Its hard to let go of the old,
And embrace the new!

Rains

A grey, wet landscape,
Raindrops on the window pane,
Raincoats, umbrellas, muddy splashes,
Windy winds,
Rains are finally here!

A parched earth,
Welcomed the rains,
Flowers blooming,
Crops flourishing,
Finally the rains are here!

The wait was long and lonely,
Like an abandoned lover,
The land waited to feel the downpour,
The rain came finally,
And meeting was worth the wait!

Will you stay long?
Asked the earth to the pregnant clouds,
Long enough to fulfil your needs,
The rains are here to stay,
And the earth is washed anew,
Like a woman in the flush of love!

Too late!

Too late
With obvious references to a late star.......
She looked into the mirror,
A stranger looked back at her.
Who is this, she whimpered,
I think I have seen her before!

She used to be a star,
Now she is a starving beggar,
The world ran behind her,
Now she is out in the cold!

She was a Queen Bee,
Till the rat race got to her,
She died alone in a room,
With no one to care for her.

They called her mad, demented,
She had lost it, they said,
Said the famous director,
I had wooed her once.

She was admired and loved,
When she was young and beautiful,
She has now been discarded,
Like a used cloth!

[We can never be sure,
Of how good we are,
Unless someone tells us so,
But the world is so busy,
With its own worries and cares,
That they forget to tell you so,
Until its too late!]

A White Lie!

A white lie!
A white lie is a good thing,
Sometimes it doesn't pay to be too honest,
No matter how good you are,
Someone is sure to strike you down !

So hide behind that mask,
Life is a masquerade,
Truth, innocence, and honesty,
Is always suspect!

It's a cynical world,
Full of subtle trickery,
No one takes you at face value,
Everyone thinks you have an axe to grind!

So watch your words,
There are many snakes in the undergrowth,
Waiting to sink their venomous fangs into you,
Lest you sail smoothly into the sunset!

Does he love me?

He loves me, loves me not!
Do you want me,
Do you love me?
I felt vulnerable,
I felt exposed!

Would he ridicule me,
Would he reject me,
What if he said,
He didn't love me at all,
Would it break my heart into a thousand pieces!

I stood before him,
Feelings naked,
The sun set in the distance,
And there was darkness all around!

Soon the moon peeked out from behind the clouds,
And there was hope,
A gentle kiss planted on my silent waiting lips,
And I knew that all was well!

The Oyster and the Pearl

The world feels like my oyster,
But someone said I wouldn't get the pearl,
I stood by the shore,
Watching the waves wash over,
Wondering what treasures it would get for me,
From the dark mysteries of the deep ocean!

I had stood by the shore,
Many moons ago,
Battered, bruised, and broken in spirit,
I had questions in my tormented soul,
I picked up an abandoned shell from the sand,
A deafening silence met me at the other end!

Today I stood there once again,
The sun went down the horizon,
A strong wind gushed around me,
Soothing me with its gentle touch.
Blowing my soft hard against my face!

A crimson glow flooded the sky,
The seagulls returned home,
To their safe havens,
The pearl I found not,
But a warm glow of fulfilment enveloped me just the same!

A new awakening!

I walked down the road,
I trod everyday,
I noticed the crimson flowers on the tree,
The young mother saying good bye,
To her toddler going to school.

I noticed the small temple in the corner,
The beggar sweeping it's courtyard,
I patted my old friend,
Who had lost her son in an accident.

I noticed the vegetable vendor,
His young son learning the tricks of the trade,
I noticed the sun rising in the horizon,
And realised it was morning!

I walked the road everyday,
But today was different,
I had been in a daze all these days,
Drowning in my own sorrows!

I noticed the world around me,
Other folks, their joys and sorrows,
Things that had been around forever,
And I realised that mine were not all!

A new awakening dawned,
A weight lifted from my shoulder,
Embrace the world as your own,
And your miseries will seem smaller!

Unseen and Unheard

So much genius around,
Languishing in the dark,
Anonymous,
unseen and unheard!

The desert rose,
Was not meant to die,
Unnoticed in the desert,
Amidst thorns and scorching heat.

A vision of the eternal truth,
That lies hidden and buried.
A vision of brilliance,
Makes life worth living.

Truth is beauty,
Beauty is truth,
Never was there more wisdom,
In such simple lines.

The system doesn't care about genius,
It cares about commerce,
Greed, power, and money,
Rule the day!

Is there any sense,
In the ramblings of my mind,
Or am I just another loser,
Beaten by the system.

Festival

The clang of cymbals,
The chant of priests,
The psychedelic lights,
The din in the neighbourhood.

The long winding queue to the *pandal*,
The coconut *jaggery* sweet,
The *pooja thali* being passed,
The collective faith of the people.

I stared at the deity,
Looked hard into her piercing eyes,
The vermillion on her forehead,
The menacing trident in her hand.

Why am I here?
I want something from you,
The crowd moved around me,
And I was in a trance.

The crowd moved away,
I stood transfixed,
In a dream like state,
The *prasad* in my hand.

The outer world ceased to exist,
A light flashed within me,
A connection with the divine power,
And I was transported.

I woke up with a jerk.
The *pandal* was empty,
The sweeper swept the grounds,
A stray dog licked my hand,
It was another day!

A stranger in the crowd!

I was screaming to be heard,
Every inch of my body in pain,
The world noticed me not,
And I was lost in the crowd.

They walked towards me,
And looked me up and down,
Who are you and,
What do you want?

I felt like an oddity,
A stranger in their midst,
A feeling that I didn't belong,
Crept over me.

I desperately wanted to fit in,
To be liked and accepted,
But I was a stranger in the crowd,
A misfit in the world!

Son of God-awful poetry fortnight!

The dog peeing on the lamp-post,
The crow shitting on the ledge,
The fat man farting in the bus,
A man's gotta do what a man's gotta do!

The ugly woman with warts on her face,
The old bent witch with gnarled fingers,
The ugly hyena going after its prey,
Its the law of the jungle here!

Nature can be pretty sometimes,
And sometimes downright ugly,
Some things are so distasteful,
We can't take a second look!

April the cruelest month

April are u cruel?
I would definitely say so,
Nor are u the beginning,
Neither the end,
You are somewhere in the middle,
Neither finished,
Just half done!

The journey has begun,
They say well begun,
Is half done!
But I am confused and lost!
I have lost my way,
Neither can I go back,
Nor race forward.

Stuck in the middle,
Neither here, nor there,
It's kinda complicated,
I am full of fear,
Oh, April! You are cruel,
Giving me no answers,
Offering no solutions to my problems!

Memories

The shaded lamp on the bedside table,
The clothes strewn on the rug,
The dog gnawing at the door,
All remind me of us.

The his and her towels in the bathroom,
The mess we'd leave there,
The bedroom slippers under the bed,
All remind me of you.

The lamp is languishing somewhere,
The dog is dead and gone,
The pottery chipped and broken,
The clothes now neatly stacked.

That was the time of our lives,
Now we are apart,
Time has gone by,
And the distance between us long.

The slimy reptile, u or me??

I stood in front of the mirror,
The bulb in the loo burned bright,
I stood admiring my pretty face,
And a lizard stood admiring me!

Its beady glassy eyes,
Stared at me,
Cold and unseeing,
Its muddy coat shimmering in the light!

It looked at me,
I stared back, repulsed,
I looked at the face in the mirror,
Then at the motionless reptile on the wall.

I saw not the bumps and warts in the mirror,
I saw only the ugly reptile,
I saw not the scars,
Only the lizard in all its glory!

Just a memory!

Are u just a photograph on the wall,
or something more?
A sum total of memories,
Of days filled with laughter and sunshine!

Are u more than just a still frame?
Or a memory of a powerhouse and a human dynamo,
This photograph dosen't do justice,
Or is it that u have paled in my heart?

I remember the days in your lap,
when u laughed at my toothless smile,
I remember holding on to your finger,
When i feared getting lost in the crowd.

I remember turning to u for advice,
When the prince i loved turned to a frog,
I remember u giving me away,
As the matrimonial fire burned bright.

I remember the tears and the joys,
And your rock solid support,
I remember the wise twinkling eyes,
The creases on the forehead,
And the grey on the temple.

The photograph dosen't do u justice,
U were such a moving force,
Enveloping us in the warmth of your embrace,
Shielding us from the storms!

Glossary of terms

Prem Kahani-Love story

Khwaaish-desire

Shaadi se Pehle-before marriage

Shaabd-words

Kajra-re-Eyes decorated with kohl

Umrao Jaan-remake of a popular film of the same name, which portrayed the life of a famous courtesan.

Aloo-parathas-Indian bread filled with mashed potatoes

Cholas-chickpeas

Thalis-a big plate of steel used for having meals in Indian

KANK-a popular Indian film Kabhi Alvida na kehna, which means never say goodbye.The film dealt with the subject of infidelity. Payjama-kurta-an Indian dress for men

Munna Bhai MBBS-a hit Indian film, wherein the central charachter, was a doctor and a bit of a gangsta!

Page 3-A term used in India to denote all the socialites who feature on a particular page of the newspaper.

Pooja-prayer

Swastik-an Indian religious symbol

Babul-name of a popular film starring Amitabh Bachchan , which means father.

Mehandi-henna applied on the hand.

Tantriks-quacks in India who pose as religious men who have strange and miraculous healing powers!Babas-same as above, *sadhus.*

Yagyas-religious ceremonies in India around the sacred fire.

Biadi-farewell of the bride when she leaves her fathers home.

Gandi-baat-impure matter

Karma-the Indian philosophy of birth and rebirth

OBC-other backward class[the caste system in India]

Baby Khoobsurat-beautiful child.

Tamasha-chaos and mayhem

Baap-father

Papad-poppadum, an eatable.

Achar-pickle

Saas-bahu-Mother-in –law and daughter-in-law

Ghar-ki –izzat-upholder of moral values at home.

Surya namaskar-a yogic pose invoking the Sun God.

Kamal-lotus

LaDame Sans Merci-the woman without mercy,[a french term]

Rakhi-an Indian festival, wherin the sister ties a thread signifing filial love on the brother's wrist.

Dhaba-an eatery where u get local food.

Kuch Kuch Hota hai-something something happens,[a popular hindi film]

Kal Ho na Ho-If tomorrow comes or does'nt.[a popular Hindi film starring heartthrob Shahrukh Khan]

Arth-meaning,[a path breaking Hindi film dealing with extra marital relations]

Iski Topi Uske Sarr-a popular hindi saying, meaning his cap on the other's head.

Shaadi Ka Ladoo-the sweet called marriage.

Teej-an Indian festival wherein the womenfolk pray and fast for their husbands wellbeing.

Karva Chauth-another similar festival, when the women break the fast after they see the moon in the sky.

Sada suhagaan-blessing given to Indian women to stay married forever

Maidan- empty ground used for playing or for festival pandals

Goondagiri-behaving like a gangsta

Taare- zameen –pe-A hit Indian film starring tyhe popular actor Amir Khan, which means stars on the ground, which dealt with specially challenged children.

Dhak-dhak-the beating of the heart

Dola-re-dola-a term used to signify a dance move.

Ek-do-teen-one two three, a popular Hindi film song.

Piya-ghar-aaya-beloved comes home.[a poplular song number featuring the reigning actress of the 90's, Madhuri Dixit]

Lakshman-rekha-a term from the Indian epic Ramanayan, which meant a married woman's boundaries.

Aksar-often, a Hindi film starring Emraan Hashmi a popular actor.

Aawarapan-Bohemianism

Zeher-poison

Kalyug-an Indian term for the bad period of humanity.

Aashiq banaya Aapne- literally meaning, you made me a lover.

Aamir-leader

Kala bandar-black monkey

Jalebi-an indian sweet which is round, orange and dipped in syrup.

Aks-a popular Amitabh Bachchan film.

Rang-de-basanti-A popular Indian film in which the youth of today questioned the system and their struggle.

Thecha-a chutney made of red chilles

Jowar rotis-Indian bread made of a kind of flour.

Pandal-a makeshift hall made of trampaulin and bamboos.Jaggery-a kind of sweet made from sugarcane extracts.

Prasad-the holy food given with blessings.

Chaat-an Indian savoury snackTikkis-potato cutlets.

About the Author

Sonal is a freelance writer based in Maharashtra, India, who has worked as a journalist for various publication houses.She is a post graduate in Literature and has a diploma in Women's studies too. She is a keen observer of life and loves to write about things she sees around her, such as societal trends, books, movies and fashion. She also writes some fiction, short stories and poetry.She writes from the heart and says it as it is without mincing words!Her world is one which you and me inhabit and she writes about things we relate to.Human relationships and emotions are important to her and this comes through in her books.She is gifted with deep sensibilities and writes sensitively about issues relating to women, youth and the common man.Her work is contemporary, set in the modern times and she makes an attempt to chronicle our changing times. Based in India, she writes about a society that is in transition,in conflict with the traditional and the modern, and a country which is fast emerging as a world power. She believes India's time under the sun is truly here, and she represents the voice of the modern, urban Indian woman. Whichever part of the world you belonged to,you would want to discover her country , through her eyes as she takes you through its myriad complexities, its problems , social issues, its icons, its great economic progress and ofcourse, you cant miss it, Bollywood! India is madness, mayhem, spirituality and salvation at the same time.Belonging to a generation of young educated Indians who have seen the transitional India, grappled with it, she becomes a voice to hear and contend with.